| | DATE DUE | | |
|---|---|---|---|
| | | | |
| | | | |
| | | | |
| | | | |
| | | | |
| | | | |
| | | | |
| | | | |
| | | | |
| | | | |
| | | | |
| | | | |
| | | | |

BLAIRSVILLE SENIOR HIGH SCHOOL
BLAIRSVILLE, PENNA.

# Life Out of Focus
Alzheimer's Disease and Related Disorders

THE ENCYCLOPEDIA OF
PSYCHOLOGICAL DISORDERS

Senior Consulting Editor Carol C. Nadelson, M.D.
Consulting Editor Claire E. Reinburg

# Life Out of Focus
## Alzheimer's Disease and Related Disorders

Dan Harmon

CHELSEA HOUSE PUBLISHERS
Philadelphia

*The ENCYCLOPEDIA OF PSYCHOLOGICAL DISORDERS provides up-to-date information on the history of, causes and effects of, and treatment and therapies for problems affecting the human mind. The titles in this series are not intended to take the place of the professional advice of a psychiatrist or mental health care professional.*

**Chelsea House Publishers**
Editor in Chief: Stephen Reginald
Managing Editor: James D. Gallagher
Production Manager: Pamela Loos
Art Director: Sara Davis
Director of Photography: Judy L. Hasday
Senior Production Editor: Lisa Chippendale

**Staff for PSYCHOLOGICAL EFFECTS OF COCAINE AND CRACK ADDICTION**
Editorial Assistant: Lily Sprague, Heather Forkos
Picture Researcher: Sandy Jones
Associate Art Director: Takeshi Takahashi
Designer: 21st Century Publishing and Communications, Inc.
Cover Design: Brian Wible

The ChelseaHouse World Wide Web site address is
http://www.chelseahouse.com

Second Printing

9 8 7 6 5 4 3 2

Library of Congress Cataloging-in-Publication Data

Harmon, Dan.
Life out of focus: Alzheimer's disease and dementia / by Dan Harmon.
  p. cm. — (Encyclopedia of psychological disorders)
Includes bibliographical references and index.
Summary: Discusses the nature, possible causes, effects on the patient as well as family and friends, and treatment options of this deteriorative disease.
ISBN 0-7910-4896-9
1. Alzheimer's disease—Juvenile literature.  2. Dementia—Juvenile literature.
3. Alzheimer's disease—Patients—Family relationships—Juvenile literature.
[1. Alzheimer's disease.  2. Diseases.]  I. Title.  II. Series.
RC523.H37          1998                                    98-26537
616.8'31—dc21                                              CIP
                                                           AC

# CONTENTS

# PSYCHOLOGICAL DISORDERS AND THEIR EFFECT

**CAROL C. NADELSON, M.D.**
PRESIDENT AND CHIEF EXECUTIVE OFFICER,
**The American Psychiatric Press**

There are a wide range of problems that are considered psychological disorders, including mental and emotional disorders, problems related to alcohol and drug abuse, and some diseases that cause both emotional and physical symptoms. Psychological disorders often begin in early childhood, but during adolescence we see a sharp increase in the number of people affected by these disorders. It has been estimated that about 20 percent of the U.S. population will have some form of mental disorder sometime during their lifetime. Some psychological disorders appear following severe stress or trauma. Others appear to occur more often in some families and may have a genetic or inherited component. Still other disorders do not seem to be connected to any cause we can yet identify. There has been a great deal of attention paid to learning about the causes and treatments of these disorders, and exciting new research has taught us a great deal in the last few decades.

The fact that many new and successful treatments are available makes it especially important that we reject old prejudices and outmoded ideas that consider mental disorders to be untreatable. If psychological problems are identified early, it is possible to prevent serious consequences. We should not keep these problems hidden or feel shame that we or a member of our family has a mental disorder. Some people believe that something they said or did caused a mental disorder. Some people think that these disorders are "only in your head" so that you could "snap out of it" if you made the effort. This type of thinking implies that a treatment is a matter of willpower or motivation. It is a terrible burden for someone who is suffering to be blamed for their misery, and often people with psychological disorders are not treated compassionately. We hope that the information in this book will teach you about various mental illnesses.

The problems covered in the volumes in the ENCYCLOPEDIA OF PSYCHOLOGICAL DISORDERS were selected because they are of particular importance to young adults, because they affect them directly or because they affect family and friends. There are individual volumes on reading disorders, attention deficit and disruptive behavior disorders, and dementia—all of these are related to our abilities to learn and integrate information from the world around us. There are books on drug abuse that provide useful information about the effects of these drugs and treatments that are available for those individuals who have drug problems. Some of the books concentrate on one of the most common mental disorders, depression. Others deal with eating disorders, which are dangerous illnesses that affect a large number of young adults, especially women.

Most of the public attention paid to these disorders arises from a particular incident involving a celebrity that awakens us to our own vulnerability to psychological problems. These incidents of celebrities or public figures revealing their own psychological problems can also enable us to think about what we can do to prevent and treat these types of problems.

# ALZHEIMER'S DISEASE: AN OVERVIEW

Think for a moment about all the places you have been, the people you have met, and the good times you have shared. Can you imagine what life would be like if you had never done any of those things or met any of those people? Take it a step further: think about everything you have learned—even the simplest things: names of objects, such as "chair" or "book," for example. Now imagine that you can no longer access that information—it has been "unlearned." If this happened to you, chances are you would feel very lonely, very confused, and very afraid.

Sadly, there are an estimated five million people in the United States who feel exactly this way. They are the victims of a terrible disease called Alzheimer's, which strips away a person's memory and experiences, changes that person's personality, and eventually prevents him or her from doing even simple tasks without help. It is the most common of a group of disorders that affect the elderly, known collectively as "senile dementia," that share many of the same characteristics. Alzheimer's is a progressive disease; this means that the condition continues to get worse over five to ten years.

Alzheimer's disease is listed as the cause of more than 100,000 deaths a year. Statistics show it is the fourth-leading killer among the adult population. It accounts for roughly half the admissions to nursing homes in the United States. The Alzheimer's Association estimates that American society spends an estimated $100 billion a year in Alzheimer's-related costs, and the federal government spent nearly $350 million on Alzheimer's research in 1998. But the greatest cost may be the emotional toll the disease takes on the families of Alzheimer's victims. More than seven out of ten people with Alzheimer's disease live at home, and almost 75 percent of the home care is provided by family and friends.

This book provides information about what, exactly, Alzheimer's disease is. It examines the possible causes of Alzheimer's, its effect on the person who is afflicted with the disorder and on family and friends around him or her, and the current methods of treating the disease.

Unfortunately, there is no way to cure Alzheimer's disease; however, with continued research efforts, someday scientists may be able to counter or eliminate the effects of this dreaded killer.

*Alzheimer's disease affects the brains of older people. The disorder gradually causes a loss of memory, leaving its victims confused and unable to care for themselves.*

# 1

# TWO FRIENDS

The following story is about two friends, Helen and Mary, who were brought together because of the terrible disease that struck them both: Alzheimer's. It is sad, but it illustrates a problem that will probably affect a friend or loved one of yours someday. Most people's lives will be touched somehow by Alzheimer's disease. The more we can learn about this great tragedy of American health, the better we can help the victims of Alzheimer's disease and those who live with and care for them.

## THE END OF A CAREER

Helen and her husband were looking forward to retirement. Helen, 56, was a professional financial planner. She was very intelligent, successful, and well respected in her community. At home, she and her husband especially enjoyed spending time with their six grandchildren. There, Helen could put numbers and finances and tax forms aside, and devote all her energy to happily spoiling the little ones.

The first sign of a problem was a gradual loss of her ability to calculate. This perplexed and startled Helen, because she had always possessed the keen mind of a mathematician. In the past, she had been able to multiply and divide large numbers in her head, and resorted to a calculator only when she wanted to show an "official" solution to one of her clients. Now, she found herself using the calculator more often.

Over the next two or three years, there were other signs that something was wrong. She had to use the calculator to solve basic math problems. Eventually, she reached the point where she wasn't even sure whether a problem called for multiplication or addition, division or subtraction. There were lapses of memory that were more embarrassing as well. Helen's mind would go blank when she started to greet certain friends by name. In time, she began

*A gradual loss of memory, affecting a person's skills and behavior, characterizes Alzheimer's disease. In Helen's case, she slowly lost her ability to calculate complex financial statements—a skill that she had developed over years as a professional. Many other talented victims of Alzheimer's have to deal with similar problems.*

having trouble getting the names of her relatives straight. She had difficulty expressing herself, finding the words to say exactly what she wanted to say. She had once been an immaculate housekeeper, but tidiness didn't seem to concern her as much anymore.

As her mental condition slowly worsened, she and her husband both worried about what was happening. Helen agreed to see a doctor for testing. The results were very disturbing. For example:

- Helen had to think hard when asked to name the president of the United States.

- When asked her age, she overstated it by several years. Then she realized the mistake and corrected herself.

- She had difficulty remembering the month of her birth.

- Providing the names and ages of her five grown children was a lengthy ordeal.

After an additional period of extensive physical and mental tests, doctors concluded that Helen was probably suffering from Alzheimer's disease. She was in good physical health, which eliminated physical causes, such as circulatory problems, an infection of the nervous system, or a brain tumor, as reasons for her mental decline. The signals clearly pointed to some form of dementia, which is a mental disorder characterized by a loss of intellectual abilities such as memory, judgment, and abstract reasoning skills, as well as by personality changes. The doctors categorized Helen's dementia as Alzheimer's.

Helen and her husband had both secretly suspected that this might be her problem, but they had never admitted their fears to each other. They returned home in shocked silence. The doctors had confirmed what they already knew: the disease was incurable. Helen's condition would slowly but inexorably get worse.

Helen began to write down her thoughts about what was happening to her. Her journal touched the hearts of everyone who read it later. "I have lost control of my life," she acknowledged. "Until a year or two ago, I could solve problems for other people. Now I cannot even prepare my own dinner without creating a disaster. My days are spent wandering and wondering."

One of her children also kept a journal. It, too, was filled with emotion: "We are watching Mom die, a day at a time."

As it turned out, Helen's husband died first, felled by a sudden heart attack. Her children, all busy professionals, hired a companion to keep an eye on Helen and make sure that she was safe. The companion, not familiar with the effects of Alzheimer's, thought it curious that Helen would sometimes speak of her dead husband as though he had only gone out to the grocery store. It was also strange, the nurse thought, that with her full wardrobe of nice clothes Helen would wear the same outfit day after day.

As Helen's mental condition grew worse, she became withdrawn and careless. She would often forget to pay monthly bills. Her deteriorating personal health and lack of toilet discipline became a problem too serious for the companion to handle. Once an attractive, well-groomed professional, Helen seemed to have forgotten all about her appearance. Perhaps the problem was that she simply couldn't remember how to dress herself properly.

In the hallway of her home hung a large mirror. Helen would often stop in front of the mirror and stare at her own image. To her, the face in the mirror seemed to be that of a complete stranger. "Who is that other woman who's staying here with us now?" she would ask her companion, sometimes several times a day. No one could convince her that the woman in the mirror was herself.

Late one night, police found Helen wandering the streets several miles from home. She was dressed in her bathrobe. She was very glad to see them, she told the officers. "Have you seen my husband? I've been looking for him everywhere. We have to find him and tell him he has a telephone call."

A year after their father's death, Helen's children decided to have her admitted full-time to an assisted-living facility. They were relieved when Helen seemed to accept the idea—at first. But when moving day came, she fought violently to remain in her home. She accused her children of driving her out against her wishes. In time, Helen became somewhat accustomed to her new surroundings. But she frequently begged to return home.

As time passed and Helen remained in the nursing home, her closest friends and family members began to look like strangers to her. Her memory loss was heartbreaking and frustrating for the people who loved her. For example, her son would enter her room.

"Who are you?" she would ask, surprised.

"I'm Arthur, your son."

"Oh, it's so good to see you. I need some water. Now!"

Arthur would return with a cup of water.

"Thank you," Helen would say, gulping it down. "Now, Mama, get me out of here. Please get me out of here."

"Mother, it's me, Arthur."

"Yes. Please get me out of here. Mama, I want to go home now."

"This *is* your home, Mother."

"No. This is not my home. Where is Daddy?"

"Dad died several years ago."

"No, he didn't. Who are you?"

Arthur would excuse himself and leave the building, blinking back tears.

## A NEW BEGINNING—A TRAGIC END

Mary was the wife of a career Air Force officer. For more than 30 years her husband Vince had been transferred from base to base around the world. She had raised their children in various areas of the United States and in several foreign countries.

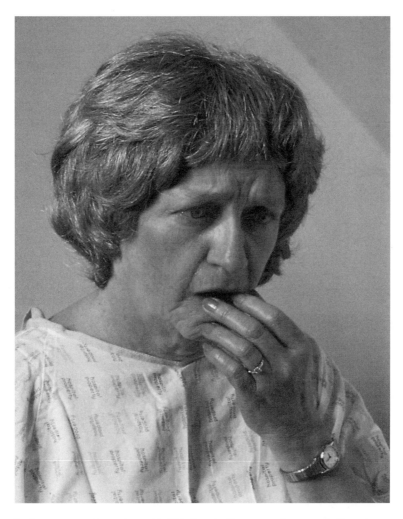

*As the memory of a patient with Alzheimer's disease continues to decline, close friends and family members may begin to look like strangers.*

The children were all grown and on their own when her husband retired from the military. This gave her a chance to pursue her favorite interest: painting. She was a greatly gifted artist, but had never had the time to study or fully develop her skills. She enrolled as a full-time student in a local art college and at age 58 she obtained her degree in art. By that time, some of her works were already being sold in galleries and exhibits.

One morning when she entered her small, cheerful studio to work, she found herself disoriented. She stared at the unfinished canvas she had intended to complete that day. It looked strange. She had no idea how she had wanted the final image to appear. Later that day, she was able to complete the painting and resume her work as if nothing was wrong. She put the troubling incident from her mind. She simply hadn't been feeling well, she told herself.

In the next few months, small incidents of forgetfulness began to add up to a changing personality. Mary would leave her studio to walk into another room of the house—and forget what she went there to do or to find. "I have too many things on my mind," she thought at first. But eventually she began to wonder what was happening to her.

Her family and friends began to notice disturbing changes in her behavior. She would forget where she had left common objects, and sometimes would confuse people's names. Sometimes her attention seemed to wander a million miles away, and the person speaking to Mary would have to call her by name or touch her shoulder to bring her back into the discussion. Mary could usually rejoin the conversation as if she had been listening all along—or could at least "fake it" so that nothing seemed amiss.

Mary had an uncanny ability to disguise her problem. Her most useful device was to change the subject when the attention turned to her. She would begin talking about a familiar topic. The change might seem abrupt to her companions, but it usually got her off the hook. One of her friends would take up the new subject of conversation, and Mary would withdraw into her private, mysterious realm of thought.

Eventually, Mary stopped trying to fake it. She would simply stare at the person who asked her a question, or would excuse herself and go to the bathroom.

When she was unable to find her parked car after shopping at a mall one day, she began to cry. A security official summoned her husband from home. That was the day Vince gently suggested she undergo a routine medical checkup. Mary knew, of course, the reason for his concern. She resisted. "There's nothing wrong with me," she told him. "I'm just getting older. We both are. We can expect things like this to happen occasionally."

But "occasionally" became "frequently" over the next two years. Her memory, orientation, and communication skills worsened. Worried friends would telephone her husband, describing Mary's dangerous driving habits

*As the disease progresses, a person with Alzheimer's will lose interest in hobbies or pastimes that were once important to him or her. This change may be difficult for that person's friends and relatives to understand.*

and her strange behavior. "She pretended she didn't even recognize me when I saw her at the supermarket," they would report.

Mary would telephone her children and friends many times a day. If they weren't home, she would leave them voice mail messages—repeatedly. On one occasion, neighbors saw her trying to drive her car while sitting in the passenger's seat!

One afternoon when Mary was home alone, her son telephoned her. He was alarmed when she failed to answer the phone, and drove quickly to her home. She was sitting in her living room, gazing blankly into the fireplace. She didn't recognize him and didn't seem to know where she was.

Mary grew increasingly impatient and agitated. When she had to wait for things to happen, she would pressure those around her to hurry—even if the situation was outside their control. No one could make her understand why certain things took time.

Supported by their children and pastor, her husband firmly insisted that she seek testing and help. By that time, test results suggested, Mary was already into an advanced stage of Alzheimer's disease. It was time for her to accept the sad news those around her already expected.

When they took away her driving privileges, it was a terrible turning point. Mary felt deprived of her freedom—in a way, of her very life. From that point, it seemed to her family that her condition worsened more rapidly.

For two more years, Mary was able to live at home. She even completed a few remarkable paintings. But she rarely finished the work she started. Her interest in art diminished. Days would pass between studio work sessions, then weeks. She stopped cooking. Her husband rarely let her walk around the neighborhood alone, because when she did she usually got lost. She required more and more assistance with her personal care and upkeep. Her husband, who was beginning to experience health problems of his own, was feeling added stress because of the situation. All of their children lived out of state and could offer little help.

Ultimately, Mary had to be admitted to a residential care facility. The decision was an emotional ordeal for her family. Surprisingly, it didn't seem to matter much to Mary at that point. She said little the day they settled her into her room, surrounded by her art and familiar mementos.

"Who painted that picture?" she asked one of her daughters, pointing.

"You did, Mother," came the choked reply.

"Oh, yes. I know. We were living in Scotland. I loved Scotland."

Her daughter hesitated, then corrected her. "No, Mom. You painted that one just a few years ago. It was while you were taking art classes at the university. Don't you remember?"

But by then her mother was ransacking the drawer of her night table. "Where are my car keys? I need to go to the supermarket. Aunt Katherine is coming today."

Aunt Katherine, her daughter knew, had died 20 years before.

*Eventually, victims of Alzheimer's disease require help with the simplest tasks, and must be moved into a nursing home or care facility where they can be overseen constantly. This is hard on family members, who may realize on one hand that they can no longer take care of their relative, while on the other hand hating the idea that their loved one is away from his or her home and surrounded by strangers.*

## FRIENDS AT THE CLOSE OF LIFE

It was at the nursing home that Mary and Helen met. They shared a table in the dining hall. For the first few months, they would talk together about art, music, flowers, and celebrities or world leaders who had impressed both of them a generation earlier. Helen, a gifted pianist, would perform in the home's common room. Mary and the other residents loved to hear her play. To a visitor, it might appear that they all were ordinary people thoroughly enjoying their latter years in the company of kindred spirits.

But on closer observation, unusual behavior became obvious. Mary and Helen would speak of long-dead relatives and friends, anticipating a visit from them shortly. Sometimes they seemed to carry on separate conversations at the same time. The response to a comment by one would be a complete change of subject by the other. To an unfamiliar observer, their conversations would make little sense. Yet Helen and Mary were relaxed and happy simply being in each other's company. They were two friends who unknowingly—or perhaps they did know— faced the same bleak end to their lives.

As they became more childlike in their behavior and less able to communicate, the relationship waned. Helen was confined to her room. It hardly seemed to matter, for she appeared unaware of where she was from day to day. Mary, too, mostly remained in her room.

During the final year of Helen's life, entries from her daughter's diary went like this:

*Friday:* Mother seems more confused each day. She thinks I am her mother, not her daughter. Most days, she believes *she* is visiting *me*! As far as she knows, she is a young girl. I think she wonders why I call her "Mother."

*Tuesday:* She usually is asleep, or dozing in and out of dreams, whenever I visit. When she is awake, she confuses her dreams with real life.

*Thursday:* All of us took mother out to dinner. We made reservations at the restaurant that used to be her favorite. She did not know where we were, but she seemed to enjoy the food and the evening. Although she did not remember the restaurant, it seemed to bring back memories of people she used to know and things they used to do together. She loved the ice cream dessert.

*Friday:* Mother begged me to take her to play golf. She hasn't played golf for at least 10 years.

*Saturday:* She didn't speak at all. I couldn't get her to answer any of my questions. So I just sat beside her bed and watched as she tossed about and stared at the opposite wall. It was as if she was asleep, suffering a bad dream. But her eyes were open.

Toward the end, there was little for her daughter to record in the diary. When she visited Helen, there was only stillness. And silence.

Helen and Mary died within a month of each other, two years after they had retired to their rooms. The immediate cause of death for both was pneumonia, which often develops when patients are bedridden for a long time. For most of their last year, they had each remained in their beds, night and day. They required total care. Neither spoke coherently to their families or to the medical staff.

In the final months, they never spoke at all. They hardly even moved.

■          ■          ■

Alzheimer's disease is a disease of the brain that generally affects older people. It is the most common of a group of disorders, known as "senile dementia," that share many of the same characteristics. As the stories above illustrate, the first signs of dementia are slight memory disturbances or subtle changes in personality. Alzheimer's is a progressive disease; this means that the condition continues to get worse with time. Usually, Alzheimer's disease gets progressively worse over five to ten years.

In the stories above, both victims of Alzheimer's disease were women. This is quite common: women are afflicted with Alzheimer's more frequently than men. It is also very common for family members to take care of a loved one with Alzheimer's for as long as they are able. The disease's greatest effect may not be on the victims, but on the estimated 12 million people who are caregivers for an Alzheimer's patient.

Alzheimer's disease is the fourth-leading killer among the adult population, causing more than 100,000 deaths each year. About half of the people admitted to nursing homes in the United States are suffering from Alzheimer's.

It's estimated that between 2 and 4 percent of Americans older than 65 have Alzheimer's disease. The percentage rises sharply as age increases. An estimated 20 percent of Americans over age 85 have Alzheimer's, notes the *Diagnostic and Statistical Manual of Mental Disorders,* fourth edition (a widely recognized authority on psychological disorders, also referred to as the *DSM-IV*). The *American Psychiatric Press Textbook of Psychiatry* suggests the rate among those older than 85 may be as high as 47 percent.

As the average age of the population increases, the percentage of Alzheimer's patients in our society will undoubtedly increase. Unless we find an effective way to treat and prevent the disease, the number of its victims is expected to nearly quadruple over the next 50 years.

Alzheimer's is a disease of the elderly: most people with the disorder are age 65 or older, and very few cases occur in people younger than 50. As a person ages, the likelihood of developing Alzheimer's disease rises. Between 20 and 47 percent of people over 85 years old are believed to have the disease.

# 2

# THE CRITICAL ISSUES: AGE AND MEMORY

Before exploring Alzheimer's disease in detail, it is necessary to understand the central, common elements it involves—age and memory. The disease is mysterious, but one thing that doctors know for certain is that it affects older people much more commonly than young adults. It was originally believed to afflict only persons in their fifties or sixties. Although some cases have been found in younger adults, Alzheimer's poses no threat for small children or teenagers.

The second factor to consider is human memory. Memory loss—one of the most obvious and distressing symptoms of Alzheimer's disease—is much more serious than forgetting the answers on a history exam or getting distracted by a TV sitcom and neglecting to finish your homework. In Alzheimer's cases, loss of memory cuts the victims off from people, places, and events that they love, essentially destroying their identities. A factor related to memory is a person's ability to learn new things. This, too, is gradually lost to Alzheimer's victims.

## EVERYONE GROWS OLD—SO WHY ALL THE FUSS?

Why are Alzheimer's and other similar forms of senile dementia such important concerns today? After all, our great-grandparents' generation did not worry much about the symptoms of dementia in older people; they regarded memory loss and personality changes as a common part of the aging process.

It's important to remember that Alzheimer's disease has come to public notice as the population has grown older. People today *expect* to live longer (and stay healthier longer) than people did a century ago. A greater percentage of our population is "old" today than in previous generations. In 1900, just one out of 25 Americans (4 percent) were past our standard retirement age, 65. By

*Senile dementia and Alzheimer's disease are important problems today in part because the overall population is getting older. About 13 percent of the U.S. population is over age 65, compared to just 4 percent a century ago.*

1998, nearly 13 percent of the U.S. population were age 65 or older. Because Alzheimer's disease typically affects older people, it's understandable that a few decades ago—when the population's average age was significantly lower—Alzheimer's wasn't recognized as a major health and "quality of life" problem, as it is now. At that time, when serious mental lapses were observed in an older person, the individual was often said merely to have grown "senile"—a condition that came to be expected in the elderly.

Today we know this pronouncement is simplistic and inaccurate. In the 1970s, great progress was made in understanding and treating physical and mental ailments common to the elderly. A major reason for the trend toward a "grayer" population is that modern science and medicine provide ways to keep people healthier and help them live longer. This has led to new emphasis in medical studies: now that more of our population is "old," scientists and doctors have a greater incentive to study the special problems of this age group and try to find medical solutions. As a result, the medical field of geriatrics, devoted to diseases of the elderly, has grown substantially.

## MEMORY: OUR IDENTITY

Our memory defines who we are. We remember certain experiences we've had, people we've known, places we've been. We forget others. Some of our memories are happy; others may make us uncomfortable or even afraid. Those memories, as the sum of our experience, determine who we are. They affect how we think. They shape many of the decisions we will make in the future.

If you lose part of your memory, you're really losing part of yourself—your identity. Stop reading for a moment and call to mind a few of your most delightful memories, some of the best times you ever had in your life. Now try to imagine what it would be like if you couldn't remember those things. You could no longer relive them. A part of your past life would be gone.

Likewise, think of two or three of your favorite people: favorite aunts or uncles, perhaps, or long-time friends. Now try to imagine how your life would be if they became complete strangers to you. Those people might still come to you and talk to you and smile and try to remind you of good times you've had together, but you would have absolutely no idea who they were or what they were talking about. Again, a big part of you will have been lost.

Memory is what holds together our lives, our identities. It connects our yesterdays with our tomorrows. It makes the whole of our lives meaningful. When the thread of memory is broken, our very identity is fragmented.

## TYPES OF MEMORY

In studying Alzheimer's disease, researchers have carefully observed its effects, not just on a person's memory in general, but on the different types of memory. Basically, there are two kinds of memory: short-term and long-term.

Short-term memory is, essentially, what we're thinking about at the moment. You can draw recollections from the past and think about them, placing them temporarily into your short-term memory. You can use short-term memory to learn a person's address or phone number, a

*This woman is a resident of a home for people with Alzheimer's disease. Because of patients' memory loss, signs have been posted as reminders of which flowers need water.*

brief quotation, or the names of a small group of people to whom you're introduced simultaneously.

Remembering this information in the future, however, involves storing it in long-term memory. Short-term memory can hold only a few items at a time—learning specialists agree that between five and nine items can be held in short-term memory simultaneously. Long-term memory, on the other hand, is like a personal "library," and it is extremely extensive. Not only can an incredible volume of information be stored in long-term memory, but it "cross-references" all this information, meaning that a person subconsciously relates certain items of information to certain other items. Thinking of a particular friend, for example, can bring to mind the memory of a trip to a theme park with that friend. You remember the roller coaster. You remember getting drenched on the log ride. You remember spilling red raspberry ice cream on your white tank top. The thought of the taste of that raspberry ice cream suddenly makes you smile. The more you think about a

# ALZHEIMER'S DISEASE: BY THE NUMBERS

Here are some interesting facts and statistics about Alzheimer's disease:

- In 1998, over 4 million people in the United States were diagnosed with Alzheimer's disease. By the year 2050, the number of people with Alzheimer's is expected to top 14 million.

- A person with Alzheimer's lives an average of eight years after the onset of symptoms.

- A national survey conducted in 1993 indicates that approximately 19 million Americans have a family member with Alzheimer's, and 37 million know someone with the disease.

- More than seven out of ten people with Alzheimer's disease live at home. Almost 75 percent of the home care is provided by family and friends. The remainder is "paid" care, costing an average of $12,500 per year. Most of this is paid for by the victim's family.

- Half of all nursing home patients suffer from Alzheimer's disease or a related disorder. The average annual cost per patient for nursing home care is $42,000; this can exceed $70,000 in some areas of the country.

- U.S. society spends an estimated $100 billion in Alzheimer's-related costs. The federal government will spend nearly $350 million on Alzheimer's research in 1998.

certain experience or place or person, the more likely it is that item will become ingrained in your long-term memory.

In between what you're thinking at this moment and what is stored in your long-term "library," your mind is at work in complex ways. A person may recall what he or she had for lunch yesterday—that information is stored in "recent" memory—but not what was eaten on Thursday two weeks earlier. There is no reason to file this information into long-term memory, unless something about the lunch was important. After a polite introduction to a stranger in a brief, casual

*One of the tragic effects of Alzheimer's is that children and grandchildren may become strangers to victims of the disease. Humans are defined, in part, by the people they know and love and by their experiences. When these things are destroyed by Alzheimer's, an important component of the person's identity is lost as well.*

encounter, you may remember the person's name for a day, a week, or a month. But if you never see the individual again, in time you will probably forget the name.

It's interesting that when Alzheimer's disease attacks, it's the loss of recent memory that's most glaringly apparent. Much of the long-term "library" seems to be still intact. The victim might remember incidents from childhood, but not what he or she did yesterday. As the disease progresses, however, the entire library of memory closes down.

Memory loss is probably the most common sign associated with Alzheimer's disease. In the initial stages of the disease, close associates may observe that the victim seems forgetful and has problems concentrating. The person is distracted easily from the topic at hand. He or she may become irritated about matters of little importance. Initially, this forgetfulness involves short-term, rather than long-term, memory. That means a person with Alzheimer's might forget a casserole left baking in the oven, but remember details of things that happened in childhood. Misplacing keys may become a regular routine. It becomes increasingly hard for the person to remember the names of familiar people.

In time, the problem becomes much more serious, and the victim's personality begins to change. An individual who once had a great sense of humor may rarely laugh at jokes anymore. A victim who once was quick at math calculations may now have unusual difficulty with numbers. This person may become noticeably confused about the time or about distances. Alzheimer's sufferers may find themselves lost when they go out walking. They forget their own birthdays, the identities of close relatives, where they used to work, where they went to college. They may exhibit changes in the way they walk and a decline in motor skills, as their bodies literally refuse to do what their brains tell them to.

## THE EFFECT ON LEARNING

We begin learning things from infancy. Science tells us that even inside the mother's womb, an unborn child is affected by—and begins responding to—sensations it experiences in its tiny world. The learning process never completely stops until we die. We can learn more things, and learn them more quickly and easily, at certain stages of our lives, but the saying "You can't teach an old dog new tricks" has been proven wrong. Countless people today are earning college degrees in their fifties, sixties, and later.

Over time, Alzheimer's disease not only erases the victim's memory, but also affects his or her ability to learn new things—even simple things. When being taken to a supermarket or doctor's office, or on a picnic to a park, the Alzheimer's patient might ask what the place is and why he or she is being brought there. A moment after hearing the explanation, the patient may ask again. And again, and again.

Dr. William Nolen, a writer and physician, says the very nature of Alzheimer's is what makes it so terrible. "Alzheimer's is a condition in which degenerative changes occur in the cortex, the upper level of the brain where the 'higher' functions—thinking, reasoning, remembering—are carried out. That's one reason why it's so scary—it affects those very activities that make us human."

*A doctor holds the medical file of the first patient diagnosed with Alzheimer's disease. The victim was a 51-year-old woman who suffered from severe loss of memory and comprehension. The disease is named for the doctor who treated her in 1906.*

# 3

# UNDERSTANDING THE DISORDER

The *American Heritage Dictionary* defines Alzheimer's as "a disease marked by progressive loss of mental capacity resulting from degeneration of the brain cells." The disease got its name from a German doctor named Alois Alzheimer, who lived from 1864 to 1915.

Doctor Alzheimer was a neurologist—a type of doctor who specializes in diseases of the nervous system. He was a pioneer in the study of the brain's structure and effects, using such materials as silver nitrate to expose the make-up of brain cells. He also examined nerve fibers and endings in the brain and central nervous system. Doctor Alzheimer was particularly fascinated by unusual nerve cells in the cerebral cortex—the part of the brain considered the site of mental functions such as memory.

In 1906, Alzheimer described a middle-aged patient who seemed to have "a peculiar disease of the cerebral cortex." This woman showed signs of progressive memory loss and a lack of orientation. She had difficulty calling people by their correct names. She believed she was being persecuted, and would hide things for no logical reason. Eventually, she became unable to move about or communicate. When she finally died, she lay cringing and helpless in her bed.

Thus "Alzheimer's disease" came to be identified, although it was not immediately known by that name. In fact, Doctor Alzheimer himself simply referred to this as a special case of "presenile dementia," or a form of dementia found in a person who is not yet elderly. (The patient was 51 years old when Alzheimer diagnosed her problem; she died at 55. Today, this would be an example of a relatively young Alzheimer's victim.) At the time senile dementia, or senility, was believed to be a regular part of the aging process. Doctor Alzheimer's report raised many eyebrows within the medical community. Because senility had been regarded as a characteristic of advancing age, most doctors in Alois Alzheimer's day believed old age

31

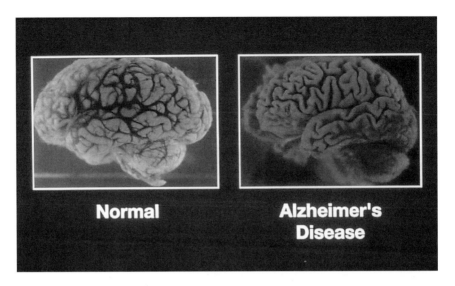

*This photo shows the differences between a healthy brain and a brain that has been damaged by Alzheimer's disease. In the latter, deep fissures in the brain, caused by atrophy, are obvious.*

which nervous impulses pass from one neuron, or nerve cell, to another; the word comes from the Greek word *synapsis*, which means "junction.") When the body does not produce enough of this vital neurotransmitter, the central nervous system does not function as well. This can lead to problems with motor skills and memory loss—scientists know that the cholinergic system, which secretes acetylcholine and similar neurotransmitters, has a great effect on memory.

## THE OUTWARD SIGNS OF ALZHEIMER'S DISEASE

Although Alzheimer's disease causes many changes in an affected person's brain, these changes cannot be seen until after a patient has died and an autopsy is performed to determine the cause of death. Doctors must diagnose Alzheimer's disease based on its physical symptoms.

According to the *DSM-IV*, two things must be demonstrated in order for doctors to diagnose dementia of the Alzheimer's type: the patient's impaired memory *and* one or more additional "cognitive disturbances." These disturbances might include aphasia (loss of the ability to communicate coherently through speech or writing or to understand language or writing), apraxia (difficulty carrying out everyday physical movements, even though the person's motor skills should be normal or unimpaired), agnosia (inability to recognize or identify common objects, although the patient seems to have normal sensory function), and/or disturbed executive functioning (problems with planning, organizing, putting things in sequence, and the like). The *DSM-IV* notes that these symptoms "each cause significant impairment in social or occupational functioning and represent a significant decline from a previous level of functioning."

Persons with Alzheimer's disease do not lose their memories and ability to think all at once. It happens over a period of months and years. In fact, the changes caused by Alzheimer's come about so stealthily in many cases that family and friends do not realize what is happening until looking back years later.

Alzheimer's has been described as the "memory-erasing disease." A common perception is that Alzheimer's patients live in abstract little worlds of their own, and that these sad domains are difficult or impossible for family and friends to penetrate. The general public thinks of Alzheimer's patients as confused, helpless individuals. But this is not necessarily accurate—not in the beginning stages of the disease, at least. Even in later stages, some patients experience extended periods of stability, welcome "plateaus" in their downward path. Doctors aren't sure why certain patients seem to be blessed with these relatively "normal" interludes, while others suffer a worsening, unrelieved course of decline.

Older adults who suffer from Alzheimer's disease are likely to deny they have a problem, or they may underestimate how seriously their memory is slipping. One study showed that people diagnosed with possible Alzheimer's were more likely to be living in denial than people who experienced simple forgetfulness as part of the aging process. Persons with "marked cognitive impairment" tended to deny their problem more strongly, compared to persons with mild impairment.

If the Alzheimer's victim is not yet retired, on-the-job problems will probably arise. The person typically becomes less productive, forcing others to assume more of the work. Failure to return telephone calls or respond to E-mail memos becomes common. The ill worker may forget appointments. Eventually, after too many no-shows and complaints from coworkers and customers, the person may be fired or asked to retire early.

# DIAGNOSTIC CRITERIA FOR DEMENTIA OF THE ALZHEIMER'S TYPE

A. The development of multiple cognitive deficits manifested by both

    (1) memory impairment (impaired ability to learn new information or to recall previously learned information)

    (2) one (or more) of the following disturbances:

        (a) aphasia (language disturbance)

        (b) apraxia (impaired ability to carry out motor activities despite intact motor function)

        (c) agnosia (failure to recognize or identify objects despite intact sensory function)

        (d) disturbance in executive functioning (i.e., planning, organizing, sequencing, abstracting)

B. The cognitive deficits in Criteria A1 and A2 each cause significant impairment in social or occupational functioning and represent a significant decline from a previous level of functioning.

C. The course is characterized by gradual onset and continuing cognitive decline.

D. The cognitive deficits in Criteria A1 and A2 are not due to any of the following:

    (1) other central nervous system conditions that cause progressive deficits in memory and cognition (e.g., cerebrovascular disease, Parkinson's disease, Huntington's disease, subdural hematoma, normal-pressure hydrocephalus, brain tumor)

    (2) systemic conditions that are known to cause dementia (e.g., hypothyroidism, vitamin B12 or folic acid deficiency, niacin deficiency, hypercalcemia, neurosyphilis, HIV infection)

    (3) substance-induced conditions

E. The deficits do not occur exclusively during the course of a delirium.

F. The disturbance is not better accounted for by another Axis I disorder (e.g., major depressive disorder, schizophrenia).

*Code* based on type of onset and predominant features:

*With Early Onset:* if onset is at age 65 years or below

> *With Delirium:* if delirium is superimposed on the dementia

> *With Delusions:* if delusions are the predominant feature

> *With Depressed Mood:* if depressed mood (including presentations that meet full symptom criteria for a major depressive episode) is the predominant feature. A separate diagnosis of mood disorder due to a general medical condition is not given.

> *Uncomplicated:* if none of the above predominates in the current clinical presentation

*With Late Onset:* if onset is after age 65 years

> *With Delirium:* if delirium is superimposed on the dementia

> *With Delusions:* if delusions are the predominant feature

> *With Depressed Mood:* if depressed mood (including presentations that meet full symptom criteria for a major depressive episode) is the predominant feature. A separate diagnosis of mood disorder due to a general medical condition is not given.

> *Uncomplicated:* if none of the above predominates in the current clinical presentation

*Specify* if:

With Behavioral Disturbance

Source: *Diagnostic and Statistical Manual of Mental Disorders,* fourth edition (*DSM-IV*).

The person may become prone to sudden, angry arguments—even physical violence. The tantrum often vanishes as quickly as it began. While the individual suffering from Alzheimer's will often resume his or her usual friendly attitude, those nearby are left confused and wondering. Interestingly, the sick person may continue to be gracious, polite, and well-mannered in public, despite the growing loss of mental abilities. Casual observers may detect nothing wrong with the person. The changed personality traits brought on by the disease may sometimes be seen only by those who come into regular contact with the sufferer.

Sleeping habits may become irregular; often the person awakes during the night and may be disoriented or prone to wander. Appetite may also change—increasing in some individuals, decreasing in others. Other symptoms that may accompany Alzheimer's disease are the three Ds: delusions, delirium, and depression. While a pattern of symptoms is common among all victims of Alzheimer's, different symptoms may seem more noticeable in different patients.

The *DSM-IV* defines four subtypes of Alzheimer's disease, depending on the "predominant feature" of the illness in any given individual:

- Dementia of the Alzheimer's type with delirium: The patient is often confused, excited, and disoriented, and experiences hallucinations.
- Dementia of the Alzheimer's type with delusions: The patient is convinced certain things are happening, when in reality they aren't.
- Dementia of the Alzheimer's type with depressed mood: Symptoms of depression are the most notable feature of the patient's condition.
- Dementia of the Alzheimer's type uncomplicated: None of the above symptoms seems to predominate.

Typically, Alzheimer's patients will eventually become unable to function without help. Often the families must admit their loved ones to a residential-care facility. As the disease approaches its conclusion, the patients become barely communicative. They don't respond to conversation or questions. They may seem unaware that another person is present. They are confined to their beds, night and day.

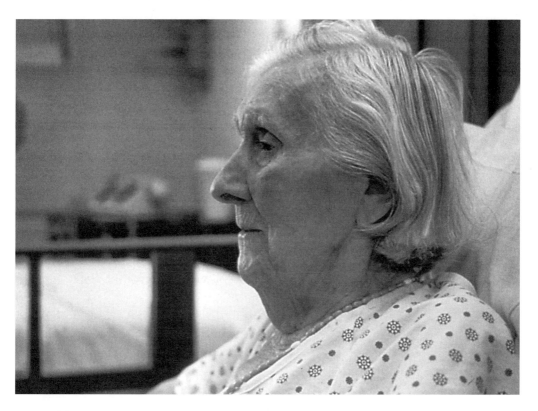

*Alzheimer's disease almost invariably changes its victims' personalities as it erases their memories and impairs their ability to think and move actively.*

Most Alzheimer's patients live 5 to 15 years after the symptoms become apparent. By the end, they seem totally adrift, alone, oblivious to the world and to the people around them. They are unable to do anything for themselves. Death seems a mercy.

It's no wonder that Alzheimer's has been called the "disease of the century." No one is immune to it.

*It is estimated that the annual cost of Alzheimer's disease to society is as high as $100 billion. The Alzheimer's Association estimates the cost of caring for the typical patient to be $175,000 over the course of the disease.*

# 4

# THE EFFECT ON SOCIETY

Among all the illnesses of modern society, Alzheimer's disease is unique. It is especially difficult for its victims and their families. Even if you are lucky enough not to know anyone afflicted with this terrible disease, Alzheimer's can still affect your life.

The monetary costs of treating and caring for Alzheimer's patients are high, but the emotional cost to families and friends may be higher. When a disoriented Alzheimer's victim steers a car into oncoming traffic and causes an accident, the effect on society is obvious to everyone. What is less obvious to everyone—but accounts for the highest toll of the Alzheimer's tragedy—is the everyday, unrelenting effect on the family and close friends of Alzheimer's victims.

## A HEAVY TOLL ON CAREGIVERS

About three-fourths of Alzheimer's patients live at home. In most cases, their family and friends take care of them. This requires a very great commitment. The demand on them is so great that their own health may suffer, in time. One study has indicated that as many as 55 percent of caregiving relatives exhibit signs of depression. Experts advise that long-term caregivers join support groups and, if necessary, seek medical assistance.

Many grown children who have a parent or parents with Alzheimer's sacrifice careers and college studies in order to devote all their time to taking care of their parent. This obviously disrupts the caregiver's own life, causing financial and emotional strains on caregiving children, their spouses, and their own children. For the person who is taking care of a parent or loved one with Alzheimer's, social activity may go out the window. "I don't have a life," is a common lament of caregivers.

*The burden of Alzheimer's may be most difficult for the loved ones of the disease's victims, especially those who try to care for the afflicted at home.*

In later stages, Alzheimer's patients require complete care. They must be bathed, dressed, and fed by others. They sometimes refuse to cooperate with—and may even physically resist—these fundamental procedures of daily life.

Often, the burdens prove too great for those trying to tend to an ill loved one at home. Caregivers have become physically ill and lost control of their own health from the stress. If they want to keep their jobs, they may have to hire daily helpers—sitters or, in more complicated cases, nursing aides. Even then, it's hard to go to work in the morning after you've spent the whole night awake with an Alzheimer's patient who wants to wander while everyone else is sleeping.

Eventually, the patient is likely to be placed in a medical care residence. The caregivers' decision to do this is extremely painful; it may bitterly divide brothers and sisters who disagree on the best care plan for their parent. As the patient becomes increasingly difficult to deal with each day, at what point do the caregivers throw in the towel and commit their loved one to institutional care? The dilemma is rarely easy to resolve.

Caregivers are often torn apart emotionally. They hurt on behalf of the victim they love so much. It hurts when your mother can't remember your name. It hurts when you see someone completely lose interest in a hobby or a cause that you know meant the world to that person before the disease progressed. It hurts to watch a loved one embarrass herself around others with inexplicable behavior—like taking off her sweater in a warm public library or church service . . . and then unbuttoning her blouse and kicking off her shoes, too. It hurts to see your grandmother cry when she realizes she isn't the same person she used to be. It hurts to see her stare at a wall. It hurts to witness the hopelessness of her condition.

The people who suffer from the effects of Alzheimer's disease, as well as the people who care for them, are often hurt by the attitudes and remarks of an uneducated public. Many people who have learned just enough about the disease to draw hasty conclusions incorrectly assume that Alzheimer's victims are completely oblivious to the world around them. For all practical purposes, they believe, these patients may as well be dead. Daily caregivers know better. Even in advanced stages, they know that they must be sensitive to their patient's needs and feelings. They realize that it is wrong to assume it doesn't matter what clothes a person wears, or what food is prepared, or what places the individual is taken to visit. Although the person may have "lost" much of his or her previous life, life still matters.

When their loved one dies, the family members are often filled with remorse. They remember the many times they became angry when the person did or said irrational things. They wish they had not said certain things—and they regret other things they never said. They wonder what they might have done differently to make life easier. They wonder whether they placed their parent or spouse into a nursing home before it was really necessary.

Although they were fighting a losing battle all along, they will always wonder if they made the right decisions for their loved one at the right times.

# THE COST OF ALZHEIMER'S DISEASE

As you can imagine, Alzheimer's disease is very expensive. The cost of medical care for its victims is only one part of the total cost. Alzheimer's also results in a loss of productivity while sufferers remain on the job, which means their employers are unable to produce as many goods, or must provide poorer services. And when this forces victims to retire early or be fired, and forces caregivers to quit their own jobs in order to tend to their loved ones who have Alzheimer's, the result is billions of dollars a year in lost wages.

Altogether, it's estimated the disease may cost victims, caregivers, employers, and others the staggering amount of up to $100 billion each year. Most of the cost must be absorbed by the patients and their families, because to a large extent health insurance and Medicare do not cover the kinds of care required. The cost each year is estimated to be almost $50,000 for the average patient; the Alzheimer's Association estimates that during the course of the disease the cost for a typical patient will be about $175,000. The only illnesses that are more costly in the United States are heart disease and cancer.

Medical professionals recommend that victims and their families obtain financial counseling because of the substantial expenses they will face. They also recommend legal counseling. It is best to deal with delicate legal issues that will arise later while the person diagnosed with Alzheimer's can still make sound and informed decisions. The legal questions that may arise include wills, advance medical directives concerning the use or removal of life support systems, participation in Alzheimer's research studies, and, at death, the performance of an autopsy. It is also important to determine who will have control over the deceased's estate. By resolving such matters early—hopefully with the patient's participation—family members can avoid additional stress and complications as the disease reaches its climax.

# ALZHEIMER'S CAN AFFECT ANYONE

In the late 1970s Rita Hayworth stood on a Broadway stage, trying without success to remember her lines. Despite her celebrated beauty and flawless dancing skills, her "faulty memory" prevented the former movie star from using her talents on Broadway. Though some critics blamed her memory lapses on alcoholism, they were actually the first indications that the actress had Alzheimer's disease, a disorder that few people were aware of at the time.

*Education about the effects of Alzheimer's disease is important. Here, an older couple and their daughter learn about the disorder from a therapist.*

Hayworth had become a star with a fine performance in the 1939 movie *Only Angels Have Wings,* which was well received. Soon she was starring in musicals opposite some of the biggest stars of the 1940s—Fred Astaire, Gene Kelly, and Frank Sinatra among them. She danced with such poise that the graceful Astaire once named her as his favorite dance partner. During this golden period of her career, Hayworth's sparkling beauty made her a popular "pin-up queen," and she appeared on the cover of *Life* magazine four times during the decade. Hayworth led the life of a Hollywood movie diva. Her five husbands included director/actor Orson Welles and Prince Aly Khan. After her divorce from Khan, however, her popularity declined and new stars like Marilyn Monroe captured the public imagination. During the 1950s and 1960s, she made fewer movies and began to drink heavily.

Her failed attempt at a Broadway career seemed to lend substance to widespread rumors that she was an alcoholic, but in 1981 she was diagnosed with Alzheimer's disease. This diagnosis brought the first public attention to the disease. Her daughter, Princess Yasmin Khan, cared for her

# THE ANGER WALL

On the Internet there is a World Wide Web page called the "Alzheimer's Anger Wall." This is a place where Alzheimer's caregivers and patients are invited to vent their daily feelings of frustration, hopelessness, and rage. It is not a pleasant place to visit, but it serves a valuable purpose. For firsthand insights about the effects of Alzheimer's disease on society, start by reading some of the postings on the "Anger Wall" (http://www.webcom.com/susan/gstbk.html). You will quickly understand how devastating the effects of this disease are on both the victims and the people who love them.

Listen to this view of Alzheimer's disease: "I hate the fact that my mother is no longer acting like an adult, that she needs to be taken care of. . . . [W]e cannot talk about books or movies or poetry anymore. I hate the fact that she can only play very simple games, no more crosswords. I want my MOTHER back the way she was!!!!"

An anonymous writer pounds on the Wall: "BAD BAD BAD DAY!!!!!"

An Alzheimer's sufferer agonizes, "I hate it because I am not as I want to be. I hate it because my heart is tormented by destructive emotions. I cannot be what I wish—it's like a plague. I just wish I wasn't."

Another patient shouts, "I am so tired of being called crazy and having everything I say challenged!"

The partner of a person with Alzheimer's steps to the Wall, ponders, and concludes simply, "[M]aybe I shouldn't be writing on the Anger Wall—it hurts too much to be angry."

To a lost loved one, one caregiver writes poignantly, "I know you didn't plan on being a burden." Another wonders, "Will there be anything left of me when Mom is gone? I need a life!"

To both patients and caregivers, the Anger Wall is a place to release some of the turmoil inside. "I am glad I can say this here, and see it written, instead of just thinking about it," one visitor explains. "Now it is a reality, as I write through flowing tears. Thanks for the space."

mother as Hayworth's health declined in the following years. The princess became a spokesperson and fundraiser for the Alzheimer's Disease and Related Disorders Association (ADRDA), an organization that works to increase public awareness of Alzheimer's disease through education, research, and family-support activities. Khan publicized her mother's condition and brought national attention to the formerly little-known disease.

Continuing the fight against Alzheimer's disease after her mother's death in 1987, Princess Khan established the Rita Hayworth Gala, an annual celebrity event that has proved to be the most successful fundraiser for Alzheimer's disease.

The most famous victim of Alzheimer's disease is undoubtedly Ronald Reagan, who served as president of the United States from 1981 to 1989. In November 1994, almost six years after leaving office, the 83-year-old wrote a letter to the American people announcing that he had Alzheimer's disease. Ironically, 11 years earlier, during his second term in the White House, he had signed into law a proclamation naming November "National Alzheimer's Disease Month."

The Reagan family had noticed symptoms of the disease for about a year and a half before his announcement. The former president might be telling a story, for instance, and in the middle of it would become distracted and forget the conclusion. To Reagan, a professional actor before he entered politics, this was the worst kind of humiliation.

Even after acknowledging the disease, Reagan continued to do things he'd always done: spending most of each weekday in his Los Angeles office, exercising regularly, riding horses and chopping wood at his ranch, and attending dinner parties. "Some days are better than others," explained his son Michael. But the former president gradually withdrew from the schedule of overseas tours and speaking engagements he had once followed. More and more, his wife Nancy began to assume the burden of caregiver. Reagan had foreseen this would happen. "I only wish there was some way I could spare Nancy from this painful experience," he had written in his public letter.

A year after he published his letter, Reagan and his wife made another announcement. They were collaborating with the American Alzheimer's Association to create the Ronald and Nancy Reagan Research Institute. The purpose, according to one press report, was to "unite the leading scientific minds from around the world with drug and biotech companies to speed information exchange and find treatments, preventions and cures." Reagan hoped that through this institute doctors, scientists, drug companies, educators, government agencies, and others involved in Alzheimer's research would share the results of their work and eventually discover a cure for Alzheimer's disease.

RONALD REAGAN

Nov. 5, 1994

My Fellow Americans,

I have recently been told that I am one of the millions of Americans who will be afflicted with Alzheimer's Disease.

Upon learning this news, Nancy & I had to decide whether as private citizens we would keep this a private matter or whether we would make this news known in a public way.

In the past Nancy suffered from breast cancer and I had my cancer surgeries. We found through our open disclosures we were able to raise public awareness. We were happy that as a result many more people underwent testing.

They were treated in early stages and able to return to normal, healthy lives.

So now, we feel it is important to share it with you. In opening our hearts, we hope this might promote greater awareness of this condition. Perhaps it will encourage a clearer understanding of the individuals and families who are affected by it.

At the moment I feel just fine, I intend to live the remainder of the years God gives me on this earth doing the things I have always done. I will continue to share life's journey with my beloved Nancy and my family. I plan to enjoy the great outdoors and stay in touch with my friends and supporters.

*In November 1994, former president Ronald Reagan announced in a letter to the American public that he had been diagnosed with Alzheimer's disease. A year later, the Ronald and Nancy Reagan Research Institute, devoted to furthering Alzheimer's research, was established in conjunction with the Alzheimer's Association.*

Unfortunately, as Alzheimer's Disease progresses, the family often bears a heavy burden. I only wish there was some way I could spare Nancy from this painful experience. When the time comes I am confident that with your help she will face it with faith and courage.

In closing let me thank you, the American people for giving me the great honor of allowing me to serve as your President. When the Lord calls me home, whenever that may be, I will leave with the greatest love for this country of ours and eternal optimism for its future.

I now begin the journey that will lead me into the sunset of my life. I know that for America there will always be a a bright dawn ahead.

Thank you my friends. May God always bless you.

Sincerely,
Ronald Reagan

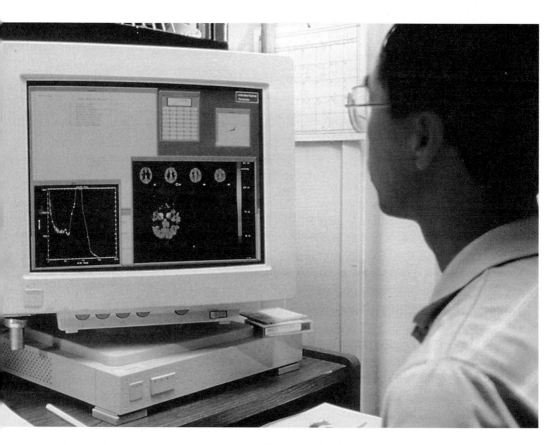

*A researcher examines a computer image of a scanned brain.*

# 5

# THE CHALLENGE OF DIAGNOSIS

How can doctors be sure they really are dealing with Alzheimer's disease? The only way to be certain is to rule out the possibility of other forms of dementia. That means doctors must first consider whether the symptoms might point to a related disorder or to a physical problem such as a brain tumor. If the doctors can rule out everything else, then they have strong basis for diagnosing Alzheimer's or indicating suspicion of the disease.

During their examination, doctors or clinicians look for problems affecting the patient's central nervous system. Conditions such as Parkinson's disease, Huntington's disease, or poor blood circulation to the brain could cause a loss of memory and other symptoms similar to those seen in Alzheimer's patients. The doctor performing the examination also looks for signs of malfunction in the various systems of the body. Shortages of Vitamin B, for example, could cause forms of dementia. So could HIV infection or hypothyroidism, a problem with the thyroid gland that causes a person to feel tired or lethargic.

Of course, these other ailments have symptoms of their own. Some of the symptoms are the same as the signs of Alzheimer's disease, while other symptoms are not commonly associated with dementia of the Alzheimer's type. Doctors have to determine whether the combined symptoms point to one disease, or possibly more than one. Clinical proof of HIV infection, impaired circulation, or permanent damage from a past head injury does not necessarily *eliminate* the possibility that the patient may have Alzheimer's disease as well.

## ALZHEIMER'S AND SIMILAR DISORDERS

We saw in Chapter 3 that Alzheimer's disease is one of many forms of dementia. Doctors must take great care in examining and diagnosing a patient with possible Alzheimer's disease. It's like a detective diligently collecting all the available evidence, then weighing the facts both individually and collectively. Doctors must determine whether the problem is Alzheimer's or something else. If the diagnosis is incorrect, the recommended plan of treatment is likely to be flawed as well.

For example, just because an elderly person suffers from both forgetfulness and bouts of depression doesn't mean the person has dementia of the Alzheimer's type. Although those symptoms are suggestive, they are only initial signs that should lead to a thorough examination. Among the factors to be considered are the probable causes of each symptom that the person shows. Has this person suffered a brain injury? Is he or she affected by cancer or by infection? Is the person abusing alcohol or drugs? Is he or she eating balanced meals? (Poor nutrition alone can produce mental irregularities.) The person's racial makeup may also have an effect on the diagnosis, as certain causes of dementia are more prevalent among some cultural groups than others. Results of this additional testing will hopefully indicate the exact nature of the person's problem.

Bear in mind that to some degree, the normal aging process is likely to bring a loss of mental faculties and physical abilities. Older people may be slow to respond to questions and may undergo changes in their ability to remember things. This is called "age-associated memory impairment." Compared to dementia of the Alzheimer's type, though, its symptoms are mild. These individuals still are able to function and, depending on their general physical health, to care for themselves. Other signs of Alzheimer's, such as marked declines in math and language skills, are not apparent.

## TESTING FOR ALZHEIMER'S

Various forms of mental tests are used to help pinpoint the disorder. They include the Wechsler Memory Scale and Wechsler Adult Intelligence Scale, the Graphomotor Alternation Test, and the California Proverb Test. Special tests have been constructed to determine possible mathematical, vocabulary, and judgment problems.

Examiners can test a patient's memory by giving the subject a word list, for example. The person is asked to repeat the words and later to recall the word list. The examiners know that providing clues such as multiple-choice questions will not help patients who have trouble learning new information. However, such prompts do help patients

*An older couple receives word about Alzheimer's disease from their doctor. An extensive period of testing must be held to rule out other possible causes for the symptoms of Alzheimer's.*

whose primary problem is memory retrieval—that is, they have learned the new information, but have trouble accessing it in their memories. Doctors also test the person's ability to remember things that were once of great interest to the person (sports, the arts, or politics, for example). This indicates the condition of the patient's long-term memory.

The clinician or doctor can gauge the patient's language abilities by pointing to objects—basic body parts like eyes or shoulders, items around the room like lamps or magazines, or photographs of common, everyday things such as fire hydrants—and asking what they are. The patient may be asked to repeat phrases, or to follow simple instructions such as "point to the window, then to the door." This type of testing also can demonstrate possible agnosia (inability to recognize common objects), which is a symptom often seen in dementia cases.

Apraxia—difficulty understanding and carrying out common actions that involve motor skills, such as brushing teeth or stacking blocks—is another common symptom of dementia. This can be tested

*There are many tests used to determine whether or not a person is suffering from Alzheimer's disease, or from another problem. Here, the doctor asks his patient to copy a three-dimensional shape onto a piece of paper; this test helps determine the woman's grasp of distances and spatial relationships.*

simply by asking the patient to execute these motor functions. The doctors also test a patient's communications skills, to see if he or she has developed aphasia (loss of the ability to communicate coherently through speech or writing or to understand language or writing).

In addition, evaluators want to understand the person's faculty for "abstract thinking." Can they perform unusual or difficult cognitive tasks, or are they likely to try to avoid them? To test abstract thought processes and other signs of "executive functioning" (such as the ability to plan and execute sequences of actions), examiners may ask the person to describe differences or similarities between words, perform simple math calculations, state the alphabet, write a line consisting of two alternating letters, or name as many animals as they can in a given period of time.

Asking an individual to copy drawings of certain shapes and overlapping patterns can help assess the person's grasp of distances and spatial relationships.

In addition to mental examinations, various kinds of tests examine the subject's brain and nervous system to help diagnose the precise nature of a disorder. These tests, including neuroimaging, computed tomography and magnetic resonance imaging, involve scans of the brain and central nervous system. Some of the scans indicate physical changes or damage to brain tissue; others reflect the amount of brain activity that is occurring in various sections of the brain while the subject is performing different functions, such as reading aloud, performing math calculations, or putting a puzzle together.

## A QUESTION OF KNOWLEDGE?

Doctors know they must be careful when they test and evaluate individuals for Alzheimer's disease or any other form of dementia. When knowledge is tested, the person who is doing the testing assumes that the subject being tested knows certain things, or knew them before mental problems began to surface. But basic knowledge cannot be taken for granted. The *DSM-IV* cautions that people from certain backgrounds, for example, may not know the names of U.S. presidents or be able to refer to geographical locations. In some cultures people cannot give their birth date, because they simply don't celebrate birthdays.

Mental testing sometimes shows that people with lower levels of education score lower on the tests. This could reflect problems with the testing process itself (for example, unrealistic assumptions that the person should know certain kinds of information). Furthermore, some test takers are more skillful than others at covering a lack of knowledge in certain areas.

A person's level of education is often determined by his or her social status and standard of living. Later in life, if symptoms of dementia surface, this background could affect the person's test score and complicate efforts to diagnose whether the individual really suffers from a psychological disorder.

## WHAT DISTINGUISHES ALZHEIMER'S FROM SIMILAR ILLNESSES?

Dementia of the Alzheimer's type involves the gradual loss of a person's mental abilities. Some of the symptoms resemble those found in persons who have other forms of mental disorders. How can doctors be relatively sure that Alzheimer's disease truly is the problem?

The illness is characterized by gradual and continuous cognitive decline. This feature distinguishes an Alzheimer's victim from a person whose symptoms, although very similar, come on suddenly or for only a limited time. For example, an accident or stroke victim might experience memory loss and other "cognitive disturbances" much like those we just described. But this is a sudden change, not a slow deterioration like Alzheimer's, and is attributable directly to the stroke or accident. The *DSM-IV* takes care to distinguish Alzheimer's cases from cases of "cognitive deficits" that should be attributed to other causes. For example:

- Certain conditions of the central nervous system cause progressive problems with memory and other thought processes. These conditions may include Parkinson's disease, Huntington's disease, and brain tumors.

- Some physical conditions can cause dementia. These include shortages or deficiencies of certain vitamins; HIV infection; and problems with the thyroid gland, which affects the body's metabolism.

- The abuse of illegal drugs, alcohol, or prescription medication is notorious for damaging a person's mental abilities.

The manual observes that to correctly diagnose dementia of the Alzheimer's type, the doctor must be able to rule out mental deficiencies that occur *only* while the person is delirious (because delirium might be brought on by any number of causes that have nothing to do with Alzheimer's disease), and other forms of mental illness that feature some of the same symptoms as Alzheimer's disease, such as depression or schizophrenia.

Diagnosing Alzheimer's disease is largely a process of elimination. Doctors often hope to discover that the patient's problem is actually one of the similar ailments mentioned above. Some of these disorders or problems, such as depression or substance abuse, can be effectively treated and the person can return to a normal life. Sadly, this is not the case of adults diagnosed with dementia of the Alzheimer's type.

## SIMILAR DISORDERS

When doctors examine an older patient who is beginning to show signs of mental deterioration, they cannot automatically and immediately classify that person as suffering from Alzheimer's disease. There are a number of other disorders—all appearing similar to Alzheimer's—that must be ruled out first.

Interestingly, the *DSM-IV* reports that the prevalence of dementia of the Alzheimer's type is higher in individuals with Down's syndrome. This is an intriguing issue to investigators, because these two ailments are quite different. Down's syndrome, described by British physician J. Langdon Down more than a century ago, is a birth defect that results in a form of mental retardation. It usually affects the sufferer's physical size and appearance as well as his or her mental abilities. Researchers have found that people with Down's syndrome who live into their thirties and forties often develop problems of the nervous system that are very similar to problems associated with dementia of the Alzheimer's type.

In the next chapter, we'll explore the issue of genetics—the theory that Alzheimer's disease may be inherited in some cases. One of the many questions scientists have explored is a possible genetic link between Alzheimer's disease and Down's syndrome. However, this is a divided issue: some studies have suggested a possible connection; others have failed to confirm any link.

Doctors have also found a higher incidence of Alzheimer's disease in people with a history of head trauma. Unlike Down's syndrome, head trauma results from physical injury after birth, rather than from a birth defect or from an inherited gene. Automobile accidents, violent crimes, and sports injuries often result in head trauma. The sport of boxing, for instance, sometimes causes a condition known as *dementia*

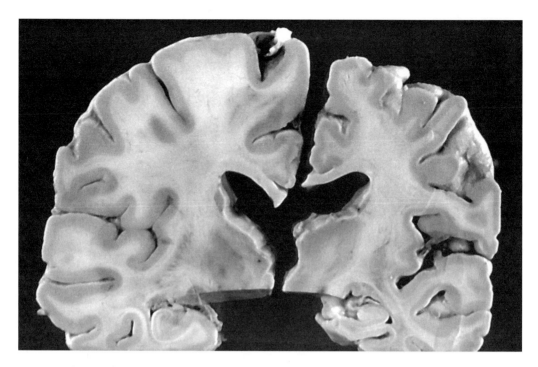

*This picture shows the abnormalities Alzheimer's disease causes in a person's brain. On the left is a normal brain from a 70-year-old; on the right is the brain of a 70-year-old person with Alzheimer's disease. Atrophy of the brain, as shown here, also occurs in disorders similar to Alzheimer's disease, such as Huntington's disease.*

*pugilistica.* ("Pugilist" is another name for a boxer.) During a fight, boxers who receive many hard blows, especially to the head, often feel "punch-drunk." They become disoriented in the ring and literally forget where they are or how to box effectively. After years of fighting, some professional boxers have been left with permanent "punch-drunk" syndrome.

Researchers have been examining the similarities between this type of condition—which includes memory loss and diminishment of higher brain function as a result of repeated head trauma—and Alzheimer's disease. However, as with Down's syndrome, the results thus far are inconclusive.

The second most common type of dementia among older people, vascular dementia, has symptoms similar to Alzheimer's. Vascular dementia is less common than dementia of the Alzheimer's type, and its onset typically occurs earlier. The disorder usually appears abruptly, and then follows a fluctuating course of rapid changes in personality, cognitive ability, and behavior, rather than the slow but steady progression of Alzheimer's. Initially, vascular dementia is commonly indicated by external neurological problems, such as difficulty walking or extreme weakness in arms or legs. It has been linked to cardiac conditions—in fact, patients suffering from vascular dementia often have a history of heart problems or hypertension—and the *DSM-IV* indicates that it may be caused by multiple minor apoplectic strokes occurring at different times. This results in damage to the brain, usually indicated by lesions in the cerebral cortex or by atrophy of various areas. As a result, the symptoms of vascular dementia can vary from patient to patient, depending on the areas of the individual's brain that are affected.

It's not uncommon for a person to be suffering from both dementia of the Alzheimer's type and vascular dementia. Doctors call this condition "mixed dementia syndrome."

Several other forms of progressive dementia often occur in older people and share many of the same characteristics as Alzheimer's disease. These include Pick's disease, Huntington's disease, and Parkinson's disease.

Pick's disease is similar to Alzheimer's disease in that it is another form of progressive dementia. Named for Czechoslovakian physician Arnold Pick, it is found most often in women between the ages of 40 and 60. Like Alzheimer's, it is characterized by memory loss and deteriorating intellect. Its victims are sometimes disoriented and emotionally unstable, and they may lose their communication skills. A key difference between this illness and dementia of the Alzheimer's type, however, is that persons suffering from Pick's disease are more likely to show only personality changes early in the course of the disease, with memory loss and orientation problems coming later.

Huntington's disease is an inherited disorder that shares many of the same features as Alzheimer's. It is marked by a progressive deterioration of thinking skills, motor skills, and emotional stability. The major difference is that the cause of Huntington's has been definitely linked to genetics: it is passed down through families through a single dominant gene that is linked to a chromosome. Children in families where one or both parents have Huntington's

## FELLING THE CHAMPION: HEAD TRAUMA AND DEMENTIA

Head injuries have been identified as causing dementia-type symptoms. One of the best examples of how continued head trauma can cause psychological problems later in life is former boxer Muhammad Ali.

"I am the Greatest!" Ali once said. Truly, he is one of the most colorful and controversial sports figures in history and arguably the best boxer of all time. Born Cassius Clay in Louisville, Kentucky, in 1942, he began boxing at age 12. After winning two consecutive National Golden Gloves tournaments, as well as a gold medal in the 1960 Rome Olympics, Clay turned pro. He moved through the heavyweight boxing ranks to become heavyweight champion by defeating the dangerous Sonny Liston in February 1964. That same year, he converted to Islam and changed his name to Muhammad Ali.

*Muhammad Ali, probably the best-known victim of Parkinson's disease, lights the Olympic flame at the opening ceremony of the 1996 Olympic Games in Atlanta.*

Ali was loud and extravagant, often bragging that no one could beat him, then backing up his words on the canvas. Between 1964 and 1967, he beat every major heavyweight contender. It seemed that nothing could take away the boxer's crown, until he was stripped of his title because he refused to register for military service at the height of the Vietnam War. It would be three years before he would be permitted to box professionally again, and four more before he regained his heavyweight title. This time, he held the title until 1978, when he lost a surprise decision to the nearly unknown Leon Spinks. He defeated Spinks in a rematch later that year to regain the heavyweight crown, then retired. "I don't want to fight no more," Ali admitted after retiring. "I've been doing it for 25 years and you can only do so much wear to the body. It changes a man. It has changed me. I can see it. I can feel it."

Despite these changes, two years later the 38-year-old attempted to make a comeback, fighting Larry Holmes and Trevor Berbick. Both fights resulted in losses. Also, both may have contributed to an alarming physical change: Ali's speech was becoming slurred and he seemed to drag his feet when he walked. The former champion tried to downplay these signs of his physical deterioration, but friends were concerned. In 1984, Ali was hospitalized for diagnostic tests to determine the cause of his worsening speech slur, listlessness, and difficulty moving. Doctors at Columbia-Presbyterian Hospital in New York City found that he was suffering from Parkinson's disease, brought about by blows to the head during his boxing career. This disclosure, and the deaths of several fighters from blows suffered in the ring, touched off a furor about boxing's role in society. The American Medical Association published a study of 38 former boxers; more than half had suffered brain damage or deteriorated tissue.

Ali is currently being treated for his Parkinson's disease with a combination of drugs that slows the disorder's inexorable advance—there is no way to stop it completely. He remains a symbol for millions, however; during the opening ceremony for the 1996 Olympic Games in Atlanta, he lit the Olympic Torch before a crowd of 80,000. Although he could not speak clearly because of his Parkinson's, the former boxer needed only to smile to remind the millions of people watching on television that he is still a champion.

disease have a 50 percent chance of developing the disorder, according to the *DSM-IV*.

Huntington's disease is usually first seen when a victim is in his or her thirties and forties, although there is a juvenile-onset form that can be seen as early as four years of age, and a late-onset type that appears as late as age 85. The disease affects men and women equally. The early signs of Huntington's are similar to those of Alzheimer's: changes in behavior and personality (such as depression, irritability, and anxiety); memory and judgment loss (especially "executive functioning"); and a decline in motor skills (this may initially be marked by increased fidgeting and will later progress to involuntary, jerky movements). As the disease progresses, the victim may suffer from disorganized speech or psychotic episodes (disturbances in perception of reality, such as delusions or hallucinations).

The disease can be identified through structural brain imaging, or positron-emission tomography (PET) scans. It is indicated by the atrophy, or wasting away, of an area of the brain called the *corpus striatum* that is part of the central nervous system. Genetic testing can also identify whether individuals at risk for Huntington's disease will actually develop the disorder; this is often done by medical centers that are experienced in counseling people and their families who are at risk for the disorder.

Like Alzheimer's and Huntington's disease, Parkinson's disease is a slowly progressive neurological condition. It is commonly marked by an uncontrollable trembling of the hands or other extremities, even when the patient is at rest. Dementia occurs in 20 to 60 percent of individuals with Parkinson's disease, and is more likely to be present in older patients, or those with more severe or advanced disease.

As with the other disorders, as Parkinson's progresses it is characterized by a loss of cognitive ability (for example, loss of memory, reduced ability to calculate or use higher thought processes, and lack of judgement regarding surroundings. And like the other forms of dementia, Parkinson's disease typically appears in older people: only 10 percent of Parkinson's patients are under age 40. However, there is a risk for younger adults, which was highlighted by the November 1998 admission by popular television and movie actor Michael J. Fox that he had quietly been battling Parkinson's for seven years, since he was 30. In a *People* magazine interview, Fox recalled how, before the 1998 Golden Globe

THE CHALLENGE OF DIAGNOSIS

Awards, he and his wife circled the event in their car several times until his medicine stopped an uncontrollable trembling in his left arm and leg. Other notable personalities that suffer from Parkinson's are 55 or older: U.S. attorney general Janet Reno, former boxing champion Muhammad Ali, and religious leader Billy Graham.

Some individuals with Parkinson's disease and dementia have been found, after an autopsy, to have the physical signs of Alzheimer's disease in the brain as well.

## TOO MUCH MEDICATION?

The use of drugs—even those prescribed by doctors for hundreds of common ailments—can produce Alzheimer's-like symptoms. In fact, drug "intoxication" is reportedly the leading cause of confusion and forgetfulness among elderly people.

In most cases, the medication is prescribed for a good reason: to combat heart disease or depression, for instance. Often, however, it produces unfortunate side effects. And these effects can linger even after the person stops taking the medicine. This is especially true with older patients: their bodily functions have slowed down, and their liver and kidneys can't expel drugs or poisons from the system as quickly as those of younger patients can.

The effects of drugs on the body can be so powerful that doctors often order their patients to stop taking all medications for a brief period if they are concerned that something else might be wrong. This helps them to determine which negative changes are caused by medication, and which ones are caused by a disease such as Alzheimer's.

■          ■          ■

As you can see, Alzheimer's researchers face a serious challenge. It's like trying to solve a jigsaw puzzle that has hundreds of pieces, while pieces of similar puzzles are constantly being tossed onto the table and scrambled among them. It's not just of question of fitting the appropriate pieces together, but of determining which pieces belong in order to solve the puzzle correctly. Yet arriving at the correct diagnosis is essential to forming a plan of care. We'll look at the options for treatment in Chapter 7.

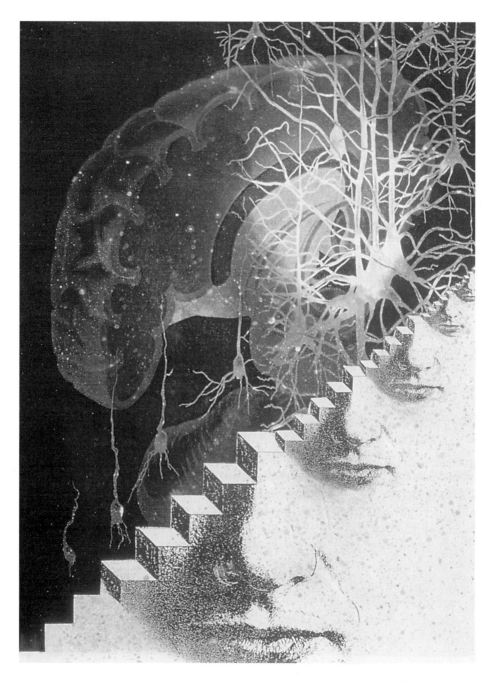

*As Alzheimer's disease progresses, its effects on a person's memory and motor skills become more severe. Doctors hope someday to determine the cause of Alzheimer's in order to better treat, or prevent, the disease.*

# 6

# POSSIBLE CAUSES OF
# THE DISEASE

To a person suffering from Alzheimer's disease, or to his or her caregivers, the cause of the disease may seem unimportant. The disease has been set in motion, for whatever reason; the damage is being done, and there is no way to stop it or even to control it very effectively.

But to medical researchers, learning the causes of diseases is vital. If the causes of a problem such as Alzheimer's disease can be found, this will assist doctors and medical professionals both in treating the disorder and in preventing others from developing it.

For researchers, one of the first questions about virtually every disease is, "Is it hereditary?" Evidence among some Alzheimer's patients suggests it may be. The *DSM-IV* reports:

> Compared with the general population, first-degree biological relatives of individuals with Dementia of the Alzheimer's Type, With Early Onset, are more likely to develop the disorder. Late-onset cases may also have a genetic component. Dementia of the Alzheimer's Type in some families has been shown to be inherited as a dominant trait with linkage to several chromosomes. . . . However, the proportion of cases that are related to specific inherited abnormalities is not known.

Another common question about the disease is, "Does a person's ethnic or cultural background have anything to do with the likelihood of the person developing Alzheimer's?" Overall, the disease seems to affect people of all races and backgrounds nearly equally, although some recent research has found that African Americans and Latinos may be more susceptible to dementia of the Alzheimer's type.

Another question researchers have considered is whether males or females are more likely to acquire the disease. The *DSM-IV* notes that

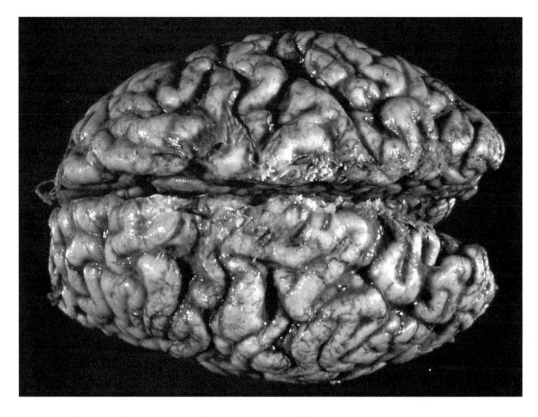

*There is evidence to suggest that many cases of Alzheimer's disease are caused by a defective gene.*

slightly more women than men suffer from Alzheimer's disease. However, this may be simply because women, on average, live longer than men.

## AN "ALZHEIMER'S GENE?"

Because there is evidence that Alzheimer's disease runs in families, researchers suspect that at least some cases of Alzheimer's are inherited. Proving the disease is genetic in certain families is difficult. Even if two or more brothers and sisters, or two or more generations of a family, acquire the disease, this does not prove that it is inherited. It might be argued that pollution of the local environment is a more likely cause, if the afflicted family members live in the same city or rural area.

However, scientists over the years have accumulated telling evidence that points to genetics, especially among early-onset Alzheimer's patients. Scientists are studying certain genes (the basic determiners of hereditary characteristics) and the chromosomes (cell structures) that carry those genes within the bodies of people with Alzheimer's disease. The researchers perform complex "linkage analyses" of the genes—that is, they study the relationship of specific genes to one another. Through linkage analysis, investigators have been able to identify the chromosomes involved in more than 100 hereditary diseases.

Chromosomes are numbered. According to a 1995 report by William Byerley and Hilary Coon, a gene associated with chromosome 14 "appears to cause the majority of early-onset Alzheimer's," while a gene on chromosome 21 seems to be involved in a small percentage of additional early-onset cases. Another gene called APOE-4 (apolipoprotein-E) is also believed to contribute to a higher incidence of the disease, at least among Caucasians. While the genes mentioned above are suspected in certain early-onset Alzheimer's cases, APOE-4 seems to affect late-onset cases.

The evidence, then, may indicate that even if Alzheimer's disease is genetic, there is not one specific gene that can be blamed as its cause. It also seems apparent that not all cases of Alzheimer's are hereditary. Altogether, research indicates slightly more than a third of all Alzheimer's cases may be "familial," or hereditary. While considering possible hereditary links, investigators have questioned such related questions as the age of the victim's mother when the victim was born, and birth-order patterns.

These findings in the area of genetics mark encouraging progress in the research battle against the disease. But they are not yet considered conclusive, and although genetic research and analysis of brain chemicals provide interesting insights into the possible causes of Alzheimer's disease, the exact cause remains unknown.

## A "SLOW VIRUS?"

Another theory is that a "slow virus" may be the biological agent that causes dementia of the Alzheimer's type. Several other diseases have been shown to be caused by slow viruses. These conditions affect the body's chemistry and destroy nerve tissue. It may take years for symptoms to develop.

The American scientist who has led the quest to identify slow viruses is Daniel Carleton Gajdusek. During the 1950s, he studied a fatal disease found among New Guinea aborigines. He was able to associate it with a virus that apparently was passed to living tribal members who devoured dead relatives' brains during a ceremony. His further research into slow viruses earned Gajdusek a Nobel Prize in 1976.

Although research into a possible viral cause for Alzheimer's is continuing, as yet there has been no virus identified as a potential cause for the disease.

## ARE THERE DIFFERENT CAUSES AMONG DIFFERENT GROUPS OF PEOPLE?

A study published in the *Journal of the American Medical Association* in spring 1998 offered two interesting results:

• Scientists found, in their test group, a higher risk of Alzheimer's disease among African Americans and Hispanics than among Caucasians.

• The possible causes of the disease (genetics, environment, and so on) may not be the same for different ethnic groups.

The study involved more than a thousand individuals over a five-year period. Some of the people under study developed Alzheimer's; others did not. Traits common to those who developed the disease and those who did not were analyzed. As we know, the likelihood of developing Alzheimer's disease increases drastically as we grow older. African Americans included in this study were shown to be four times more likely than Caucasians to acquire Alzheimer's by the time they were 90 years old. Hispanics were twice as likely to be affected as Caucasians. These rates were not affected by heredity, gender, or educational background.

Even if scientists prove different rates of likelihood of the disease among different ethnic groups, there are deeper complications to be unraveled. For example, another study indicated that native Africans in Nigeria seemed much less likely to have Alzheimer's disease than African Americans. Different eating habits were suspected as a possible factor. For instance, yams, a popular food item in Nigeria, are high in the hormone estrogen. Some researchers believe estrogen may help lower the chance of developing the disease.

*Recent research has found that African Americans and Hispanics are more likely to develop Alzheimer's disease than Caucasians. One study found that African Americans were four times as likely as Caucasians to develop the disease by the time they were 90 years old.*

More study is needed to validate the results of these studies. Dr. George Martin, a neuropathologist in Seattle, explained, "If African Americans and Hispanics have some unidentified genes that put them at further risk, we need to know what they are and how they work so we can target therapy for them."

In the past, research has determined that some types of circulatory and hypertension diseases are more common among African Americans than among Caucasians. Could there be a link—possibly suggesting a related cause—between these types of ailments and dementia of the Alzheimer's type? Researchers want to know the answer.

# OTHER POSSIBLE CAUSES

Metal poisoning is a possible factor being explored in medical research of Alzheimer's causes. For example, some studies have shown a comparatively high level of aluminum traces in the brain tissue of Alzheimer's patients. Humans come into contact with aluminum in various household products. Might regular use of those items over a lifetime lead to, or contribute to, the development of Alzheimer's disease? This is unproven so far.

Poor nutrition in childhood may be another possible cause of Alzheimer's disease. In 1998 Robert Abbott, a professor at the University of Virginia Medical School, released the results of his study of over 3,700 men, age 71 to 91, whose growth was stunted by malnutrition during childhood. Dr. Abbott found that these men were nearly three times as likely to develop memory loss and other forms of cognitive decline later in life.

Currently, researchers are also studying other potential factors that may affect the development of Alzheimer's disease, such as:

- *Problems with the body's immune system.* With increasing age, the body's immune system changes. How do these changes affect brain cells? Although Alzheimer's patients show signs of disturbance in their immune systems, evidence that this has actually *caused* the disease seems thin.

- *Permanent damage from head injuries.*

- *A family history of Down's syndrome.*

- *Problems related to the thyroid gland.*

- *Blood cancer.*

What is certain is that understanding the cause or causes of a disease is a necessary first step to finding cures and methods of prevention. Various treatments are already being tried on Alzheimer's patients, as we will discuss in Chapter 7. The closer researchers come to pinpointing the causes of this disorder, the more effective treatment programs will become.

*A medical professional cares for a man with Alzheimer's disease. A wide variety of treatment methods have been used to slow the progression of the disorder.*

# 7

# TREATMENT OF ALZHEIMER'S DISEASE

Is there a cure for Alzheimer's disease? Most doctors agree there is not: Alzheimer's is considered progressive and unstoppable. However, although Alzheimer's disease cannot be cured, medications are often prescribed to diminish the severity of some of its symptoms. When doctors prescribe these medicines, it is vital that they know for certain the identity of the disease they are treating. A medication useful in treating one form of dementia, such as Parkinson's disease, may be useless or counterproductive if the illness is Alzheimer's or a different type.

Doctors use medication to accomplish two things:

1. Diminish the person's problematic behavior (getting lost, becoming unreasonably hostile, or the like)

2. Temporarily stabilize the patient's mental abilities

Over the years, various medicines—ranging from high-potency vitamins to mental stimulants—have been tested and found unsatisfactory in treating dementia of the Alzheimer's type. Today, however, certain drugs are known to help relieve some of the symptoms. The most popular are a type called cholinesterase inhibitors.

Chapter 3 discussed the cholinergic system and noted that it has a great effect on memory. Drugs called cholinesterase inhibitors can be administered to improve, and complement, the body's production of neurotransmitters like acetylcholine. Because Alzheimer's disease appears to attack these neuro-transmitters, doctors and researchers have attempted to introduce cholinesterase inhibitors into the nervous system. In theory, this will build up the cholinergic system, undoing some of the damage caused by Alzheimer's. Efforts to enhance the performance of neurotransmitters with these drugs have, in fact, shown some success, although results have not been consistent.

The two most popular cholinesterase inhibitors are Tacrine and Donepezil; in various studies, they have been shown to improve the mental functions of some test patients. However, it is not clear why other patients involved in the tests did not show improvement with a program of cholinesterase inhibitors. The two drugs have been approved by the Food and Drug Administration for treating Alzheimer's disease. Other cholinesterase inhibitors include Physostigmine and Metrifonate.

While these drugs show promise, they can also produce unpleasant side effects. Donepezil, for instance, may cause nausea, vomiting, muscle cramps, sleep irregularity, and appetite loss. Those ailments are a small price to pay, though, for the prospect of improving Alzheimer's symptoms.

Some observers predict that efforts to protect or restore patients' neurotransmitter systems will be the focus of future Alzheimer's research. If a drug—or a combination of drugs—can guard the body's nervous system against deterioration from dementia of the Alzheimer's type, normal (or at least improved) thought patterns might be assured.

## ALZHEIMER'S AND ESTROGEN

In Chapter 6, a study was mentioned that indicated estrogen may help lower a person's chance of developing Alzheimer's disease. That study found that native Africans in Nigeria were less likely to have Alzheimer's disease than African Americans, and postulated that the Nigerians' diet, which included a high amount of estrogen-rich yams, played an important part. But what is estrogen, and why would it have an effect on a disease of the brain like Alzheimer's?

Estrogen is a hormone that is developed naturally in both the male and female human body, although it is usually considered a female sex hormone. In women, estrogen is responsible for the development of female sexual characteristics. More important, it is an essential part of the female reproductive cycle; estrogen acts on the female reproductive organs to produce an environment suitable for fertilization, implantation, and nutrition of the embryo that eventually will grow into a baby.

Around the age of 50, women stop menstruating, and their bodies no longer produce estrogen. This period is called menopause. Studies have shown that after menopause women have a higher incidence of breast cancer and osteoporosis (a loss of bone mass). As has been discussed, Alzheimer's disease also typically occurs in women over age 50—that is, postmenopausal women.

*When a woman passes through the stage of life known as menopause, the amount of the hormone estrogen her body produces is reduced sharply. Studies have found that treatment to replace estrogen in the body reduces a woman's risk of Alzheimer's.*

Estrogen replacement therapy is now common for postmenopausal women because it been found to reduce the likelihood of osteoporosis and heart disease, although it can increase a woman's risk of getting breast cancer. Estrogen replacement therapy has also been shown to have a positive effect on Alzheimer's patients. Several studies have indicated that, when given to older women, estrogen replacement therapy appears to reduce a healthy woman's risk of developing Alzheimer's disease, Parkinson's disease, or other types of senile dementia. Estrogen also seems to slow the mental decline of women who already have one of these diseases. In 1998, Dr. Sanjay Asthana of the Geriatric Research Education and Clinical Center in Seattle studied 12 women with mild-to-moderate dementia. Six of the women were given an estrogen patch, and the others were given a placebo. During the five-week study, each woman's memory, language skills, and ability to concentrate were evaluated, using standard tests. Overall, the women with the estrogen patches scored higher on the tests.

# ALZHEIMER'S AND NICOTINE

In 1996, Michael Zagorski of Case Western Reserve University found that nicotine, a drug that is found in tobacco products such as cigarettes, can slow or stop the progression of Alzheimer's disease. Zagorski studied beta peptide, a normal substance in the brain that becomes abnormal in Alzheimer's patients. The disease causes the beta peptide to clump together into solid plaques that damage brain tissue. These plaques are visible indicators of the disease when deceased Alzheimer's patients are autopsied.

Zagorski found that, under normal conditions, about 50 percent of the beta peptide taken from Alzheimer's patients would become a toxic peptide plaque. When he introduced nicotine into the beta peptide mix, however, only 8 percent mutated into plaque. Further experiments showed that, over time, the nicotine actually reversed the formation of beta peptide plaque.

Other studies have shown that nicotine improves a person's cognition. Nicotine has been found to increase acetylcholine, the important neurotransmitter that helps regulate memory, learning, and attention.

Researchers around the world are trying to create a nicotine-based drug that could be used to prevent and treat Alzheimer's disease. However, there can be no treatment until the drug's negative side effects can be countered. Nicotine may be the most addictive of all drugs; it causes a powerful psychological addiction that will drive a person to continue using the drug once he or she is "hooked." Nicotine is a naturally occurring component of tobacco, commonly smoked in cigarettes or cigars. The effects of smoking include lung cancer and emphysema, high blood pressure, heart attacks, and strokes. Chewing tobacco has other negative effects, such as oral cancer. No doctor or researcher would ever suggest that smoking cigarettes or chewing tobacco is a good way to avoid Alzheimer's disease. "I wouldn't advise anyone to start smoking," Zagorski noted in a 1996 *Newsday* article. "Smoking is hazardous to your health."

# COMBINATION TREATMENTS

Doctors have sometimes combined two or more treatment methods in an attempt to combat the effects of Alzheimer's disease. This is not uncommon in the medical world; people suffering from cancer, heart disease, diabetes, and other major illnesses are commonly treated with more than one type of medication. The strategy seems to make sense, considering that Alzheimer's may be caused or affected by a combination of factors.

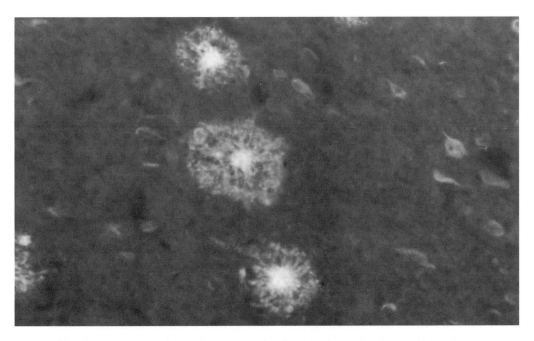

*This microscope view shows the plaques that form in the brain of an Alzheimer's patient when certain nerve cells mutate and clump together. Research has shown that nicotine can halt, and even reverse, this process. However, an effective Alzheimer's treatment involving nicotine has not yet been developed because of the drug's dangerous side effects.*

One study of a combined Alzheimer's treatment compared two groups of women. One group was given both Tacrine (a cholinesterase inhibitor) and estrogen-replacement therapy; the other was given only Tacrine. The patients who received both treatments showed greater improvements than the patients who received just the cholinesterase inhibitor.

While results like these are encouraging, they have not been conclusive. Studies with other drug combinations have indicated no great improvements by mixing medicine. More multiple-treatment studies are needed. At the moment, combined medication for dementia of the Alzheimer's type is not a standard procedure.

## TREATING THE SYMPTOMS INDIVIDUALLY

In addition to the methods used to treat the specific causes of Alzheimer's disease and preserve an afflicted person's memory, doctors

# FETAL TISSUE RESEARCH

Alzheimer's disease, like other forms of senile dementia, occurs as a result of damage to the brain's neural tissue. This tissue is different from other tissue cells in your body. If you fall and break a bone, the bone cells will eventually grow together and be as strong as before. If you cut your arm, the skin cells will regenerate and the cut will heal. However, the specialized tissue in the brain, spinal cord, and central nervous system does not have the ability to regenerate itself when it is damaged. As a result, most brain damage is permanent.

Over the years, doctors have attempted to transplant healthy neural tissue into areas where significant neural damage has occurred. However, this has proven difficult, in part because the human body often rejects foreign tissue. The body's immune system may attack the transplant, creating health complications.

To resolve this problem, researchers have attempted to replace damaged neural tissue with cells from a developing fetus. "Fetus" is the name for a developing human baby eight or more weeks after conception. In the early months after conception, the fetus grows rapidly, and its cells are very adaptable. If the fetus is aborted at eight to nine weeks old, its neural tissue can be transplanted into another person's neural system, where it will "learn" what that person's neural system needs and adapt to perform that function, thereby reversing the brain damage.

Study of aborted fetuses has taught doctors a lot about birth defects and prenatal care. Fetal tissue has also been used to test the effects of various drugs on human cells. It has been used in attempts to treat Alzheimer's disease, Parkinson's disease, Huntington's disease, and AIDS, and could someday be used in treatment of diabetes, epilepsy, optic disorders, and spinal-cord problems such as paraplegia.

However, the use of fetal tissue is highly controversial. The tissue taken from a fetus that is spontaneously (naturally) aborted is usually damaged and not very useful. The neural tissue must be removed from the living fetus, and therefore must be obtained from healthy fetuses that women choose to abort; the extraction of the tissue kills the unborn child. As a result, many people object to

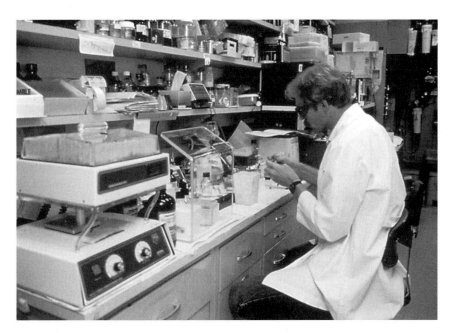

*Fetal tissue research has become a controversial issue in the search for an Alzheimer's cure. Many people object on moral grounds to the use of tissue taken from unborn children.*

use of fetal tissue on moral grounds. Some people argue against it because they believe that the unborn fetus is human, and therefore abortion is a crime against humanity. Others fear that demand for aborted fetal tissue will create a "black market," where women become pregnant in order to abort the fetus and sell the tissue for profit.

Although initial results of fetal tissue implants have been mixed, only time will tell if the transplant procedure can become part of successful treatment for Alzheimer's and other neurological diseases. However, there is no question that the debate over the ethics of fetal tissue research will continue well into the next century.

*A doctor and nurse show a box of Risperidone, an antipsychotic used to treat behavioral disturbances caused by Alzheimer's disease.*

also use other drugs to combat the specific side effects of Alzheimer's disease. For example, when given in mild dosages neuroleptic drugs (also known as "antipsychotics" or "tranquilizers") can counteract such Alzheimer's-related problems as anger or agitation, sleeplessness, and paranoia. Neuroleptic drugs have a relaxing, sedative effect on the person taking them.

Sedatives like clozapine, benzodiazepine, trazodone, and carba- mazepine also are used to diminish agitation or hostile behavior. Cloza- pine is sometimes prescribed to patients who have adverse reactions to neuroleptics, but it may produce bad side effects of its own, such as fever, nausea, and a tendency to gain weight. Benzodiazepines also carry the risk of unpleasant side effects, like drowsiness and symptoms of amnesia (forgetting one's identity)—working against the purpose of prescribing the drug in the first place.

Because many Alzheimer's patients experience disruptions in their sleep-wake cycles, sleeping pills may be prescribed for insomnia.

A study published in 1997 indicated that dosages of Vitamin E and selegiline (better known by the trade name Deprenyl) may have slowed the progress of the disease in a test group of Alzheimer's patients. Earlier, selegiline had shown promise in possibly slowing the progression of Parkinson's disease, but had been disappointing in Alzheimer's studies.

## OTHER FORMS OF TREATMENT

Overall, the use of drugs has been only partly successful in fighting Alzheimer's disease. How, for example, can any drug keep a person from wandering away from his or her home? Or make him or her pay attention and respond when spoken to? Or remember where he or she is? So in addition to medication, clinicians try to combat the disease with psychotherapy and psychosocial management.

Psychotherapy is a type of treatment for mental disorders and behavioral disturbances. Clinicians attempt to modify a person's behavior through techniques such as support, suggestion, reeducation, and reassurance, rather than through drugs. Simply listening and sympathizing when an Alzheimer's patient vents his or her frustration with the disease can be therapeutic.

In Alzheimer's cases, common psychotherapy techniques include the "three Rs:" repetition (regular reminders of what day of the week it is, or the identity of the caregiver), reassurance (low-key conversation intended simply to calm the patient), and redirection (changing the subject or perhaps taking the patient for a walk when the patient becomes frustrated or angry). Caregivers must learn to make these techniques part of their everyday lifestyle, as we'll see later in this chapter.

Other effective forms of psychotherapy are group and family support sessions, behavior modification (changing certain behavior patterns in a person through conditioning, self-esteem bolstering, and other methods), and environmental manipulation (for example, eliminating noise). A patient's sleep irregularities may be managed in part by establishing a set wake-up time each morning, controlling naps during the day, and limiting the consumption of beverages at night.

The patient's primary caregiver, naturally, is essential to the success of psychotherapy. Caregivers are encouraged to learn all they can about the disease and effective ways to manage its symptoms. The next chapter will look at some of the problems that caregivers and family members face with Alzheimer's disease.

*Alzheimer's is especially stressful for caregivers—the people who take care of an afflicted loved one.*

# 8

# COPING STRATEGIES FOR CAREGIVERS

While scientists and doctors labor to discover and prescribe the right kind of medicine, the day-to-day well-being of Alzheimer's patients depends on their caregivers. These are the people who carry out the medical program to help each sufferer. That's not nearly as simple as providing aspirin for a headache. Caregivers must administer medication at the proper time of day in order for it to work effectively. Obviously, if the purpose of a drug is to help the patient sleep, it should be given shortly before bedtime. With other kinds of medicine, deciding the best time to administer it can be complicated. For example, caregivers learn to predict daily activities (like bathing) that tend to agitate the patient; they must time the medication schedule so that the drug will take effect at the right moment and lessen the problem.

Besides ensuring that the drug achieves the best effect, accurate timing means that caregivers can administer the smallest amount of medicine necessary to give the patient the full benefits of the medication. With elderly Alzheimer's patients (as in virtually all areas of health care), the lower the dosage of medication required, the better off the patient will be.

Caregivers must constantly look for possible side effects of medication. For example, if the dosage of a sedative is too strong, the drug may actually heighten a patient's agitation—a symptom these drugs are supposed to relieve. Overmedication can make the patient groggy, possibly causing a loss of balance and a bad fall, resulting in broken bones (especially in older people) and contributing greatly to the person's health crisis. And certain types of drugs are not safe for a person who also suffers from health problems such as heart disease or diabetes. Some medications, while helpful in treating Alzheimer's if taken by themselves, can produce dangerous reactions in combination with certain other medicines the patient may be using to treat unrelated health problems.

*Although dealing with a person with Alzheimer's can be frustrating, caregivers must encourage their patients, rather than criticize them.*

The caregiver must not become so preoccupied with the person's Alzheimer's disease that he or she does not recognize other health ailments that may be affecting the patient, such as arthritis, sight or hearing loss, infections, and heart or lung problems. In addition to regular and thorough medical care, a daily routine of well-balanced meals and exercise is especially important for people suffering from dementia of the Alzheimer's type.

## HOW SOME CAREGIVERS COPE

As Alzheimer's disease pursues its steady course, week by week, month by month, the victims' lives slowly come unraveled. Many of them realize it is happening. They sense a gradual loss of mental faculties, and they understand what the final outcome will be. They watch the tragedy helplessly as it unfolds, engulfing them and their loved ones.

For family and loved ones the stress may be greater—especially if the immediate family members are the caregivers.

Caregivers learn to cope with the reality of the disease, and to do what they can for their patients. They learn to take care of things without appearing overbearing or "bossy." They learn to encourage rather than criticize, realizing that their loved ones may be struggling to communicate but have simply lost that ability. Caregivers draw from the helpful findings of previous caregivers, and they devise their own methods.

For as long as possible, they try gently to keep the individual in touch with the world around them. How? One way is through constant orientation. Moderate and advanced Alzheimer's patients may forget something that was said or done only minutes earlier. They need to be reminded what day it is, what the weather is like outside, who the caregiver or visitor is—even if he or she is a close relative.

Caregivers continually point out family photographs and describe who's in the picture. They draw the patient's attention to heirloom furniture and other long-familiar objects. They keep diaries. These things may stir the patient's memory and create feelings of peace and security. One relative of a person with Alzheimer's disease reported installing a whiteboard with washable pens on the wall beside the patient's telephone. When guests visited this woman, they would write brief notes to remind her that they had been there. They also programmed speed-dial buttons on a special telephone that she could use, and posted their abbreviated telephone speed-dial numbers on the whiteboard; for a while, the patient could phone them whenever she wanted to talk, without needing to deal with a standard seven- or ten-digit telephone number.

To help lessen the patient's confusion, some caregivers keep the home as quiet as possible. When a loved one becomes agitated, quietly reading to the patient often helps. Familiar texts seem to work best. One woman said that when she reads Bible passages to her fretful mother, "the result is nothing short of a miracle."

The same caregiver described television as "the worst culprit." Although her mother enjoyed watching some of the programs, the plots and characters—especially those from soap operas and mysteries—became confused with reality. The patient believed TV personalities were occupying her house; she couldn't understand why she was not allowed to enter the TV realm and respond to some of the things the actresses and actors were saying. There are stories of Alzheimer's patients living in daily fear of some TV or movie villain they believe to be real. A patient in her eighties went so far as to buy a gun to protect herself from a fictitious stalker she'd seen on television. Television newscasts are no better: they often present the patient with tragedy, violence, and a barrage of short interview clips showing unfamiliar faces, which can be confusing and upsetting.

Even comedy shows can lead to small problems. The caregiver above who pointed out the distraction caused by TV said her mother continued to watch her favorite sitcom—until she began noticing clothes and other items on the set that resembled her own belongings. She thought the comedy characters had raided her wardrobe!

This is not to say that television programming cannot be usefully incorporated into the care plan. Cooking programs, for example, tend to be comforting as well as informative. Wildlife and travel programs can have a similar effect—as long as they do not contain violent footage or dangerous situations. Nonviolent sports like golf or tennis can be entertaining.

When certain tactics fail, dedicated caregivers always seem willing to try something new. One reported, "It took patience—a lot of patience. It took experiments. I became like a scientist, measuring the effect of every variable in my mom's world. . . . I assessed all and set out to control every variable, cutting off the negative, turning up the positive."

An important resource for Alzheimer's caregivers is their support network. They come together in person, on the phone, and on the Internet to share advice, experiences, and tears.

Patients themselves also join support groups. Diana Friel McGowin is widely known for *Living in the Labyrinth*, the book she wrote about Alzheimer's from the patient's perspective. Devoting her time and energy to patient advocacy, she helped form an Alzheimer's disease support group for patients, which communicates via the Internet provider America Online. Patients log in to help each other cope and discuss research developments. They even find amusing things to smile about. (Diana Friel McGowin can be contacted at http://members.aol.com.LILAUTHOR1.)

Family members who are taking care of a parent or elderly relative at home must take precautions to ensure the safety of their patient. They may be forced to lock the person inside the house much of the

*Although currently there is no effective treatment for Alzheimer's, hope remains that one day a cure–or at least a way to manage and minimize the disease's effects–can be found.*

time, and build security fences outside so that the individual cannot stray from the yard and become lost. Many Alzheimer's patients wear bracelets with medical alert devices. In addition, caregivers often must unplug electrical equipment, fasten drawers and cabinets, and hide car keys in order to keep the patient from causing an accident and possibly getting hurt.

As their condition worsens, some Alzheimer's patients must be restrained to protect them from their own harmful, albeit unknowing, actions, as well as to protect others. Modern restraining devices are designed with patient comfort in mind. Some of them, for example, keep the person safely attached to a bed but allow free movement (rolling, sitting up, sitting at bedside).

## A "MANAGEABLE" DISEASE?

Professionals working to fight Alzheimer's disease believe that they could make faster progress toward a cure if more funds were provided for research. The Alzheimer's Association points out that the U.S. government spent an estimated $349.2 million for Alzheimer's research in 1998. While this seems like a large figure, Alzheimer's advocates believe this allotment is low considering the amount the disease costs society each year. The Alzheimer's Association says the government's spending on Alzheimer's amounts to just $1 for every $287 the disease currently costs society. They point out that medical research into problems such as heart disease, cancer, and AIDS receives four to seven times the amount of funding that Alzheimer's does.

Nevertheless, some researchers are optimistic. Progress in fighting the disease is slow, but there is always hope for a breakthrough. Even if no permanent cure is discovered, some doctors believe research and experimentation may soon pay off with medications that effectively "manage" the disease. Under that scenario, Alzheimer's would continue to be serious and incurable, but it would be treatable—much like diabetes or heart disease. For some patients, at least, Alzheimer's would no longer be the devastating, invincible killer it is today.

Remarkably, some Alzheimer's patients are optimistic, too. In an Internet forum in 1998, one Alzheimer's patient wrote, "Because of past lack of knowledge and misinformation many feel this is a long death sentence. I choose to see it as a time for me to get the priorities of life in order and live each moment to the fullest."

# APPENDIX

# FOR MORE INFORMATION

**Alzheimer's Association National Office**
919 N. Michigan Avenue, Suite 1000
Chicago IL 60616-1676
Phone: (800) 621-0379
Fax: (312) 335-1000
Website: www.alz.org
Information on local chapters of the
Alzheimer's Association is available
on-line or by calling the national office.

**Alzheimer's Disease Education and
Referral Center (ADEAR)**
ADEAR Center, Box 8250
Silver Spring, MD 20907-8250
Phone: 800-438-4380 or (301) 459-3311
Website: www.Alzheimers.org

**Alzheimer's Society of Canada**
1320 Yonge Street, Suite 201
Toronto, Ontario M4T 1X2
Phone: (416) 925-3552
Website: www.alzheimer.ca/alz

**American Geriatrics Society**
770 Lexington Avenue, Suite 300
New York NY 10021
Phone: (212) 308-1414
Fax: (212) 832-8646
Website: www.americangeriatrics.org

**American Medical Association**
515 North State Street
Chicago, IL 60610
Phone: (312) 464-5000
Website: www.ama-assn.org

**National Alliance for the Mentally Ill**
200 N. Glebe Road, Suite 1015
Arlington, VA 22203-3754
Phone: (800) 950-6264
Fax: (703) 524-9094
Website: www.nami.org

**National Institute on Aging**
Information Office
9000 Rockville Pike
Building 31, Room 5C35
National Institutes of Health
Bethesda MD 20892
Phone: (301) 496-1752
Website: www.nih.gov/nia

**National Family Caregiver Association**
9621 East Bexhill Drive
Kensington, MD 20895-3104
Phone: (800) 896-3650
Fax (703) 684-5968
Website: www.mediconsult.com/
associations/nfca

**National Mental Health Association**
1021 Prince Street
Alexandria, VA 22314-2971
Phone: (800) 969-6642
Fax (703) 684-5968
Website: www.aoa.dhhs.gov/aoa/dir/
181.html

# APPENDIX

# NATIONAL ALZHEIMER'S DISEASE CENTERS

The National Institute on Aging currently funds 28 Alzheimer Disease Centers at medical schools around the country. Activities vary from center to center, from the molecular biology of Alzheimer's disease to programs that support caregivers.

## Alabama

Lindy E. Harrell, M.D., Ph.D., Professor
Department of Neurology
University of Alabama at Birmingham
1720 7th Ave. South
Sparks Center 454
Birmingham, AL 35294-0017
(205) 934-9775
fax: (205) 975-7365

## California

William J. Jagust, M.D., Director
Alzheimer's Disease Center
University of California, at Davis
Alta Bates Medical Center
2001 Dwight Way
Berkeley, CA 94704
(510) 204-4530
fax: (510) 204-4524

Jeffrey L. Cummings, M.D., Professor
Department of Neurology and Psychiatry
University of California at Los Angeles
School of Medicine
710 Westwood Plaza
Los Angeles, CA 90095-1769
(310) 206-5238
fax: (310) 206-5287

Leon Thal, M.D., Chairman
Department of Neuroscience (0624)
University of California at San Diego
School of Medicine
9500 Gilman Dr.
La Jolla, CA 92093-0624
(619) 534-4606
fax: 534-1437

Caleb E. Finch, Ph.D.
Division of Neurogerontology
Ethel Percy Andrus Gerontology Center
University of Southern California
University Park, MC-0191
3715 McClintock Ave.
Los Angeles, CA 90089-0191
(213) 740-1758
fax: (213) 740-0853

## Georgia

Suzanne Mirra, M.D., Professor
Dept. of Pathology and Laboratory Medicine
Emory University School of Medicine
VA Medical Center (151)
1670 Clairmont Rd.
Decatur, GA 30033
(404) 728-7714
fax: (404) 728-7771

## Illinois

Denis A. Evans, M.D., Professor of Medicine
Rush Alzheimer's Disease Center
Rush-Presbyterian-St. Luke's Medical Center
1645 West Jackson, Suite 675
Chicago, IL 60612
(312) 942-3350
fax: (312) 92-2861

Robert E. Becker, M.D.,
Center for Alzheimer Disease and
    Related Disorders
Southern Illinois University School of
    Medicine
751 North Rutledge
P.O. Box 19230
Springfield, IL 62794-1412
(217) 785-4468
fax: (217) 524-2275

## Indiana

Bernardino Ghetti, M.D., Professor of
  Pathology, Psychiatry, and Medical
  and Molecular Genetics
Indiana Alzheimer's Disease Center
Department of Pathology, MS-A142
Indiana University School of Medicine
635 Barnhill Dr.
Indianapolis, IN 46202-5120
(317) 274-1590
fax: (317) 274-4882

## Kansas

William C. Koller, M.D., Ph.D.,
  Professor and Chairman
Department of Neurology
University of Kansas Medical Center
3901 Rainbow Blvd.
Kansas City, KS 66160-7117
(913) 588-6952
fax: (913) 588-6965

## Kentucky

William Markesbery, M.D., Director
Sanders-Brown Research Center on Aging
University of Kentucky
101 Sanders-Brown Bldg.
800 South Lime
Lexington, KY 40536-0230
(606) 323-6040
fax: (606) 323-2866

## Maryland

Donald L. Price, M.D., Professor of
  Pathology, Neurology, and Neuroscience
Johns Hopkins University School of
  Medicine
558 Ross Research Bldg.
720 Rutland Ave.
Baltimore, MD 21205
(410) 955-5632
fax: (410) 955-9777

## Massachusetts

John H. Growdon, M.D.
Department of Neurology
Massachusetts Alzheimer's Disease
  Research Center
Massachusetts General Hospital
WAC 830
15 Parkman St.
Boston, MA 02114
(617) 726-1728
fax: (617) 726-4101

## Michigan

Sid Gilman, M.D., Professor and Chair
Department of Neurology
Michigan Alzheimer's Disease Research
  Center
University of Michigan
1914 Taubman Center
Ann Arbor, MI 48109-0316
(313) 936-9070
fax: (313) 936-8763

## Minnesota

Ronald Petersen, M.D., Ph.D., Assoc.
  Professor
Department of Neurology
Mayo Clinic
200 First St. SW
Rochester, MN 55905
(507) 284-2203
fax: (507) 284-2203

## Missouri

Leonard Berg, M.D.
Alzheimer's Disease Research Center
Washington University Medical Center
The Health Key Bldg.
4488 Forest Park Blvd.
St. Louis, MO 63108-2293
(314) 286-2881
fax: (314) 286-2763

## New York

Michael Shelanski, M.D., Ph.D., Director
Alzheimer's Disease Research Center
Dept. of Pathology
Columbia University
630 West 168th St.
New York, NY 10032
(212) 305-3300
fax: (212) 305-5498

Kenneth Davis, M.D., Professor and Chair
Dept. of Psychiatry
Mount Sinai School of Medicine
Mount Sinai Medical Center
1 Gustave L. Levy Place, Box #1230
New York, NY 10029-6574
(212) 241-6623
fax: (212) 996-0987

Steven Ferris, Ph.D.
Aging and Dementia Research Center
Dept. of Psychiatry (THN314)
New York University Medical Center
550 First Ave.
New York, NY 10016
(212) 263-5703
fax: (212) 263-6991

Paul Coleman, Ph.D., Professor
Dept. of Neurobiology and Anatomy
Box 603
University of Rochester Medical Center
601 Elmwood Ave.
Rochester, NY 14642
(716) 275-2581
fax: (716) 273-1132

**North Carolina**

Allen Roses, M.D., Dir. and Principal
   Investigator
Joseph & Kathleen Bryan Alzheimer's
   Disease Research Center
2200 Main St., Suite A-230
Durham, NC 27705
(919) 286-3406
fax: (919) 286-3228

**Ohio**

Peter Whitehouse, M.D., Ph.D., Dir.
Alzheimer's Disease Center
University Hospitals of Cleveland
11100 Euclid Ave.
Cleveland, OH 44106
(216) 844-7360
fax: (216) 844-7239

**Oregon**

Earl Zimmerman, M.D., Chair
Dept. of Neurology (L-226)
Oregon Health Sciences University
3181 S.W. Sam Jackson Park Road
Portland, OR 97201-3098
(503) 494-7321
fax: (503) 494-7242

**Pennsylvania**

John Trojanowski, M.D., Ph.D., Professor
Dept. of Pathology and Laboratory Medicine
University of Pennsylvania School of
   Medicine
Room A-009, Basement, Maloney/HUP
36th and Spruce Sts.
Philadelphia, PA 19104-4283
(215) 662-6921
fax: (215) 349-5909

Steven DeKosky, M.D., Director
Alzheimer's Disease Research Center
University of Pittsburgh Medical Center
Montefiore University Hospital, 4 West
200 Lothrop St.
Pittsburgh, PA 15213
(412) 624-6889
fax: (412) 624-7814

**Texas**

Stanley Appel, M.D., Director
Alzheimer's Disease Research Center
Dept. of Neurology
Baylor College of Medicine
6501 Fanning, NB302
Houston, TX 77030-3498
(713) 798-6660
fax: (713) 798-7434

Roger Rosenberg, M.D., Director,
   Alzheimer's Disease Research Center,
   Zale Distinguished Chair, and Professor
   of Neurology and Physiology
University of Texas Southwest Medical
   Center at Dallas
5323 Harry Hines Blvd.
Dallas, TX 75235-9036
(214) 648-3239
fax: (214) 648-6824

**Washington**

George Martin, M.D., Professor
Alzheimer's Disease Research Center
Dept. of Pathology
Box 357470, HSB K-543
University of Washington
1959 N.E. Pacific Ave.
Seattle, WA 98195-7470
(206) 543-5088
fax: (206) 685-8356

# APPENDIX

# BIBLIOGRAPHY

American Psychiatric Association. "Delirium, Dementia, and Amnestic and Other Cognitive Disorders." In *Diagnostic and Statistical Manual of Mental Disorders*, 4th ed. Washington, D.C.: American Psychiatric Press, 1994.

———. *Practice Guideline for the Treatment of Patients with Alzheimer's Disease and Other Dementias of Late Life.* Washington, D.C.: American Psychiatric Press, 1997.

Byerley, William, and Hilary Coon. "Strategies to Identify Genes for Schizophrenia." *American Psychiatric Press Review of Psychiatry*, volume 14. Edited by John M. Oldham and Michelle B. Riba. Washington, D.C.: American Psychiatric Press, 1995.

Check, William A. *Alzheimer's Disease.* Philadelphia: Chelsea House Publishers, 1989.

Edelson, Edward. *Aging.* Philadelphia: Chelsea House Publishers, 1990.

Houlihan, David, Benoit Mulsant, Robert Sweet, A. Hind Rifai, Rona Pasternak, Jules Rosen, and George Zubenko. "A Naturalistic Study of Trazodone in the Treatment of Behavioral Complications of Dementia." *American Journal of Geriatric Psychiatry* 2, no. 1 (Winter 1995).

Johnson, Keith A., and J. Alex Becker. *The Whole Brain Atlas* (CD-ROM), 1998. An electronic version is available online at http://www.med.harvard.edu/AANLIB/home.html.

Kumar, Anard, Andrew Newberg, Abass Alari, Paul Moberg, Jesse Berlin, David Miller, Elaine Souder, Raquel Gur, and Gary Gottlieb. "MRI Volumetric Studies in Alzheimer's Disease." *American Journal of Geriatric Psychiatry* 2, no. 1 (Winter 1995).

Li, Ge, Jeremy M. Silverman, Christopher J. Smith, Michele L. Zaccario, James Schmeidler, Richard C. Mohs, and Kenneth L. Davis. "Age at Onset and Familial Risk in Alzheimer's Disease." *American Journal of Psychiatry* 152, no. 3 (March 1995).

Malaspina, Dolores, H. Matthew Quitkin, and Charles A. Kaufmann. "Epidemiology and Genetics of Neuropsychiatric Disorders." In *American Psychiatric Press Textbook of Neuropsychiatry*, 2nd ed. Edited by Stuart Yudofsky and Robert E. Hales. Washington, D.C.: American Psychiatric Press, 1992.

Masterman, Donna L., Ann H. Craig, and Jeffrey L. Cummings. "Alzheimer's Disease." In *Treatments of Psychiatric Disorders*, 2nd ed. Edited by Glenn O. Gabbard. Washington, D.C.: American Psychiatric Press, 1995.

Samuels, Steven C., and Kenneth L. Davis. "Experimental Approaches to Cognitive Disturbance in Alzheimer's Disease." *Harvard Review of Psychiatry* 6, no. 3 (May–June 1998).

Schulte, Brigid. "'African Americans, Latinos more likely to contract Alzheimer's,' study finds." Knight Ridder Newspapers, 12 March 1998.

Sevush, Steven, and Nancy Leve. "Denial of Memory Deficit in Alzheimer's Disease." *American Journal of Psychiatry* 150, no. 5 (May 1993).

Silverman, Jeremy M., Ge Li, Michele L. Zaccario, Christopher J. Smith, James Schmeidler, Richard C. Mohs, and Kenneth L. Davis. "Patterns of Risk in First-Degree Relatives of Patients with Alzheimer's Disease." *Archives of General Psychiatry* 51, no. 7 (July 1994).

Talan, Jamie. "Study: Nicotine Could Block Alzheimer's." *Newsday* 23 October 1996.

Wartik, Nancy, and Lavonne Carlson-Finnerty. *Memory and Learning*. Philadelphia: Chelsea House Publishers, 1989.

Weiner, Myron F., Richard C. Risser, C. Munro Cullum, Lawrence Honig, Charles White III, Samuel Speciale, and Roger N. Rosenberg. "Alzheimer's Disease and Its Lewy Body Variant: A Clinical Analysis of Postmortem Verified Cases." *American Journal of Psychiatry* 153, no. 10 (October 1996).

Wise, Michael G., and Kevin F. Gray. "Delirium, Dementia, and Amnestic Disorders." In *American Psychiatric Press Textbook of Psychiatry*, 2nd edition. Edited by Robert E. Hales, Stuart C. Yudofsky, and John A. Talbott. Washington, D.C.: American Psychiatric Press, 1994.

Yesavage, Jerome, John Brooks, Joy Taylor, and Jared Tinklenberg. "Development of Aphasia, Apraxia, and Agnosia and Decline in Alzheimer's Disease." *American Journal of Psychiatry* 150, no. 5 (May 1993).

# APPENDIX

## FURTHER READING

American Psychiatric Association. *American Psychiatric Press Textbook of Psychiatry*, 2nd ed. Washington, D.C.: American Psychiatric Press, 1994.

———. *Diagnostic and Statistical Manual of Mental Disorders*, 4th ed. Washington, D.C.: American Psychiatric Press, 1994.

———. *Practice Guideline for the Treatment of Patients with Alzheimer's Disease and Other Dementias of Late Life*. Washington, D.C.: American Psychiatric Press, 1997.

———. *Treatment of Psychiatric Disorders*, 2nd ed. 2 vols. Washington, D.C.: American Psychiatric Press, 1994.

Check, William A. *Alzheimer's Disease*. Philadelphia: Chelsea House Publishers, 1989.

Edelson, Edward. *Aging*. Philadelphia: Chelsea House Publishers, 1990.

Grubbs, William. *In Sickness and In Health: Caring for a Loved One with Alzheimer's*. Forest Knolls, Calif.: Elder Books, 1996.

Markin, R. E. *Coping with Alzheimer's: The Complete Care Manual for Patients and Their Families*. Secaucus, N.J.: Citadel Press, 1998.

McGowin, Diana Friel. *Living in the Labyrinth: A Personal Journey Through the Maze of Alzheimer's*. New York: Delta, 1994.

Orr, Nancy K., Steven Zarit, and Judy M. Zarit. *The Hidden Victims of Alzheimer's Disease: Families Under Stress*. New York: New York University Press, 1985.

Pollen, Daniel A. *Hanna's Heirs: The Quest for the Genetic Origins of Alzheimer's Disease*. New York: Oxford University Press, 1996.

Rozelle, Ron. *Into That Good Night*. New York: Farrar, Straus & Giroux, 1998.

Smoller, Esther Strauss, and Kathleen O'Brien. *I Can't Remember: Family Stories of Alzheimer's Disease*. Philadelphia: Temple University Press, 1997.

Strecker, Teresa R. *Alzheimer's: Making Sense of Suffering.* New York: Vital Issues Press, 1997.

Tappen, Ruth M. *Interventions for Alzheimer's Disease: A Caregiver's Complete Reference.* Baltimore: Health Professions Press, 1997.

Thomas, Clayton C., ed. *Taber's Cyclopedic Medical Dictionary*, 15th ed. Philadelphia: A. Davis Company, 1985.

Wartik, Nancy, and Lavonne Carlson-Finnerty. *Memory and Learning.* Philadelphia: Chelsea House Publishers, 1989.

# APPENDIX

# GLOSSARY

**Agnosia:** Inability to recognize common objects. Agnosia is a symptom often seen in dementia cases.

**Alzheimer's disease:** A progressive disease that has a degenerative effect on the brain, causing severe dementia. Initial signs of the disease are slight memory disturbance or subtle changes in personality; the disease progresses slowly but inexorably over the next 5 to 10 years until the person is completely disoriented. There is no cure.

**Aphasia:** Loss of the ability to communicate coherently through speech or writing or to understand language or writing. Aphasia is a symptom common in Alzheimer's patients.

**Apraxia:** Difficulty understanding and carrying out common actions that involve simple motor skills, such as brushing teeth. Apraxia is a common symptom of dementia.

**Choline:** A vitamin, produced naturally by the body, that prevents deposits of fat in the liver and is essential in transmission of nerve impulses through the synapses of the brain and central nervous system. A lack of this vitamin can negatively affect a person's memory.

**Cholinesterase inhibitors:** Drugs used to build up a person's cholinergic system and enhance the performance of neurotransmitters. These drugs—including Tacrine, Donepezil, Physostigmine, Galanthamine, and Metrifonate—have been approved by the Food and Drug Administration (FDA) to treat Alzheimer's disease.

**Dementia:** A mental disorder characterized by a general loss of intellectual abilities, such as impairment of memory, judgment, and abstract thinking. It is often accompanied by changes in personality. Alzheimer's disease is the most common cause of dementia.

**Down's syndrome:** A chromosome disorder that occurs in the developing fetus and results in physical changes and moderate to severe mental retardation. Researchers have found that people with Down's syndrome develop problems of the nervous system that are very similar to problems associated with dementia of the Alzheimer's type.

**Head trauma:** A wound or injury to the head, such as from an accident or from repeated blows, as in a boxing match. A history of head trauma may affect the occurrence of Alzheimer's disease or related disorders.

**Huntington's disease:** An inherited disorder, similar to Alzheimer's, that usually appears in adults age 30–40. The early signs of Huntington's are similar to those of Alzheimer's: changes in behavior and personality (such as depression, irritability, and anxiety); memory loss; and a decline in motor skills (this may initially be marked by increased fidgeting and will later progress to involuntary, jerky movements). As the disease progresses, the victim may suffer from disorganized speech or psychotic episodes (disturbances in perception of reality, such as delusions or hallucinations).

**Long-term memory:** Memory that is retained over a long period of time.

**Parkinson's disease:** A slowly progressive neurological condition that is commonly indicated by an uncontrollable trembling of hands or other extremities, even when the patient is at rest. Dementia occurs in 20–60 percent of individuals with Parkinson's disease.

**Pick's disease:** Like Alzheimer's disease, a form of progressive dementia. It differs from Alzheimer's in that brain atrophy is confined to the frontal and temporal lobes; while Pick's disease is characterized by memory loss and deteriorating intellect, a key difference between this illness and dementia of the Alzheimer's type is that persons suffering from Pick's are more likely to show only personality changes early in the course of the disease, with memory loss and orientation problems coming later.

**Psychotherapy:** A type of treatment for mental disorders and behavioral disturbances. Clinicians attempt to modify a person's behavior through techniques such as support, suggestion, reeducation, and reassurance, rather than through drugs.

**Short-term memory:** Memory that is lost within a brief period unless reinforced. Learning specialists have concluded that a person can have between five and nine items in short-term memory at one time.

**Synapse:** Connection point in the central nervous system at which nervous impulses pass from one nerve cell to another. The word comes from the Greek word *synapsis*, which means "junction."

**Vascular dementia:** A disorder that is similar to Alzheimer's disease but is linked to cardiac problems; people suffering from vascular dementia often have a history of heart disease. Although it is the second most common type of dementia among older people, it is much less common than Alzheimer's. The disorder is caused by a series of small strokes; it usually appears abruptly and then follows a fluctuating course of rapid changes in personality, cognitive ability, and behavior, rather than the slow but steady progression of Alzheimer's. The disease typically appears in younger people than does Alzheimer's. It is sometimes called multi-infarct dementia.

# APPENDIX

# INDEX

# APPENDIX

# PICTURE CREDITS

Page

8: AP/Wide World Photos

10: R.T.Nowitz/Photo Researchers, Inc.

12: © Junebug Clark/Photo Researchers, Inc.

15: Photo Researchers, Inc.

17: © Blair Seitz/Photo Researchers, Inc.

19: ADEAR, National Institute on Aging, N.I.H.

22: ADEAR, National Institute on Aging, N.I.H.

24: ADEAR, National Institute on Aging, N.I.H.

26: R.T.Nowitz/Photo Researchers, Inc.

28: AP/Wide World Photos

30: AP/Wide World Photos

33: ADEAR, National Institute on Aging, N.I.H.

34: ADEAR, National Institute on Aging, N.I.H.

39: ADEAR, National Institute on Aging, N.I.H.

40: © NIH/Science Source/Photo Researchers, Inc.

42: ADEAR, National Institute on Aging, N.I.H.

45: ADEAR, National Institute on Aging, N.I.H.

48: AP/Wide World Photos

49: AP/Wide World Photos

50: ADEAR, National Institute on Aging, N.I.H.

53: ADEAR, National Institute on Aging, N.I.H.

54: (top) Photo Researchers, Inc.; (bottom) © Will & Deni McIntyre/Photo Researchers, Inc.

58: © Biophoto Associates/Science Source/ Photo Researchers, Inc.

60: AP/Wide World Photos

64: Hans-Ulrich Osterwalder/Science Photo Library/Photo Researchers, Inc.

66: © Martin M. Rotker/Science Source/Photo Researchers, Inc.

69: ADEAR, National Institute on Aging, N.I.H.

72: ADEAR, National Institute on Aging, N.I.H.

75: ADEAR, National Institute on Aging, N.I.H.

77: ADEAR, National Institute on Aging, N.I.H.

79: ADEAR, National Institute on Aging, N.I.H.

80: AP/Wide World Photos

82: AP/Wide World Photos

84: © Will & Deni McIntyre/Photo Researchers, Inc.

87: © Bill Aron/Photo Researchers, Inc.

**Senior Consulting Editor Carol C. Nadelson, M.D.,** is president and chief executive officer of the American Psychiatric Press, Inc., staff physician at Cambridge Hospital, and Clinical Professor of Psychiatry at Harvard Medical School. In addition to her work with the American Psychiatric Association, which she served as vice president in 1981–83 and president in 1985–86, Dr. Nadelson has been actively involved in other major psychiatric organizations, including the Group for the Advancement of Psychiatry, the American College of Psychiatrists, the Association for Academic Psychiatry, the American Association of Directors of Psychiatric Residency Training Programs, the American Psychosomatic Society, and the American College of Mental Health Administrators. In addition, she has been a consultant to the Psychiatric Education Branch of the National Institute of Mental Health and has served on the editorial boards of several journals. Doctor Nadelson has received many awards, including the Gold Medal Award for significant and ongoing contributions in the field of psychiatry, the Elizabeth Blackwell Award for contributions to the causes of women in medicine, and the Distinguished Service Award from the American College of Psychiatrists for outstanding achievements and leadership in the field of psychiatry.

**Consulting Editor Claire E. Reinburg, M.A.,** is editorial director of the American Psychiatric Press, Inc., which publishes about 60 new books and six journals a year. She is a graduate of Georgetown University in Washington, D.C., where she earned bachelor of arts and master of arts degrees in English. She is a member of the Council of Biology Editors, the Women's National Book Association, the Society for Scholarly Publishing, and Washington Book Publishers.

**Dan Harmon** is an editor and writer living in Spartanburg, South Carolina. He has written several books on humor and history, and has contributed historical and cultural articles to the *New York Times, Music Journal, Nautilus,* and many other periodicals. He is the managing editor of *Sandlapper: The Magazine of South Carolina* and is editor of *The Lawyer's PC* newsletter. His books in the Chelsea House series THE ENCYCLOPEDIA OF PSYCHOLOGICAL DISORDERS include *Anorexia Nervosa: Starving for Attention* and *The Tortured Mind: The Many Faces of Manic Depression.*